Sewing for Mini Dolls

Sherralyn St. Clair

COPYRIGHT

Copyright 2017 Sherralyn St. Clair

You may sell or give away as many of the dolls or the doll clothing as you can make by yourself. The dolls or clothing cannot be mass produced without my permission. You may make as many copies of the patterns as you need for your own use. You may not give away or sell the patterns or the instructions, or kits containing the patterns or instructions.

V 17-09-12

ISBN-13: 978-1976027734

ISBN-10: 197602773X

ABOUT THE FRONT COVER

Free instructions for Twinkle's insect net can be found at www.sherralynsdolls.com. Select Florabunda's page from the buttons at the top of the main page. On Florabunda's page select easy craft projects from that page's directory.

INTRODUCTION

American Girl® Dolls has recently changed the body of their American Girl mini doll, and Target now sells Our Generation® mini dolls and Lori® mini dolls. I have changed my Twinkle doll pattern slightly to more nearly match these dolls and have revised my mini doll clothing patterns to give them a better fit on these new dolls. The older mini dolls can still wear these revised patterns, but be sure to check the fit on an older doll before securing the elastic or adding hook and loop tape to back closings.

I have added new patterns to this book so that it offers a more complete doll wardrobe than the first edition. I have also added accessories and extras to make the book more fun; simplified the shoe patterns; added new touches to patterns that were in the book's first edition; rearranged the patterns and chapters to make the book easier to use; and added more instructions to the book based on questions from readers. The key to the symbols used in the patterns and instructions now appears on the next page.

Many of my readers have tried to use this book to teach their children and grandchildren to sew. I did not intend this book for children. Using a sewing machine to make items as small as mini doll clothing can be challenging for the beginner. At first I considered including simplified handsewing patterns in this book. I found that the book's format became too complicated with the addition of the simplified patterns. I am working on a separate book of simplified doll clothes patterns that I hope to publish soon after this revised book is in print. You can find many easy patterns in this new mini doll book, but if you need something for the complete beginner look for my new book, about handsewing for mini dolls.

Email me at sherralyn@sherralynsdolls.com if you haves questions, suggestions, or just want to chat about dollmaking.

Symbols

Symbols Used in the Book's Instructions and Patterns

- The pattern pieces for mini doll clothing in this book are marked by an open star (☆)..
- **Tips** p (page number) refers you to the page in the appendix, **Tools, Tips, and Techniques**, that contains additional information about the sewing project.
- In these instructions light gray indicates the right side of the fabric.

- In these instructions white indicates the wrong side of the fabric.

- In the patterns a dashed line indicates a sew line.
- In the patterns a thick broken line indicates where to gather the fabric.
- In the patterns a closely spaced dotted line indicates topstitching.
- In the patterns a line with two dots and a dash indicates staystitching.
- In the patterns a widely spaced dotted line indicates where to fold the fabric after cutting.
- In the patterns and these instructions the location of clips is indicated by a small scissor icon and a gray line.

CONTENTS

Nightgown, Undies, and Socks..7

A mini doll can be well dressed from the inside out, beginning with the patterns and instructions from this chapter. Make panties, tights, a camisole, half slips, and socks. Make a nightshirt, nightgown, or both for bedtime.

Separates..15

A mini doll can have a typical kid's wardrobe with all the mix and match choices from this chapter. Make long pants or shorts. Use jean or khaki fabric for casual pants, if you like. Make an A-line or two tiered skirt. Patterns for adding optional pockets to the pants and A-line skirt are included. Tops include a T-shirt, pull-over sweater, smock, and summer top. A short jacket can be used with the T-shirt and summer top from this chapter and the A-line dress and sundress from the next chapter.

Dresses...29

You can use your imagination to embellish the dresses in this chapter. Add pockets or appliques to the A-line dress and sundress. Use interesting cotton prints or just your favorite colors for the A-line, sundress, or classic dress. Use silky fabric and metallic lace for a royal ballgown and add lace to the neck and hem of the classic dress or ballgown, if you like. You can add ribbon or trim to the fitted waist of these last two dresses.

Coats..41

The raincoat and the winter coat use the same pattern. Fabric choice and fasteners give a different look to each coat. The robe can be worn over the nightgown or nightshirt.

Extras...49

The extras in this book are here to add extra fun to doll dressing, doll collecting, and doll play. The collection of footwear includes shoes, bunny and mouse slippers, sneakers, and boots. Hats include a nightcap, a rain or sun hat, and a princess crown. Totes include a purse and a backpack. This chapter ends with instructions for a working umbrella and an all cloth doll bed with its bedding.

Twinkle Doll..69

Use this pattern to make your own mini doll. The pattern includes optional details like tiny fingers and toes. As an option there are instructions explaining how to prepare and print a fabric sheet with faces

Spoonflower® Custom Printed Fabric..83

You can order fabric printed with the mini Twinkle doll face, head, and body, instead of using the patterns in the book. If you are interested, this chapter will tell you how to order it from Spoonflower® and how to use the fabric to make Twinkle dolls. The chapter also contains information about fabric printed with mini doll sneaker and slipper patterns.

Tools, Tips, and Techniques...87

This appendix provides additional details for some of the sewing techniques and procedures used in the patterns.

Nightgown, Undies, and Socks

A mini doll can be well dressed from the inside out beginning with the patterns and instructions from this chapter. Make panties, tights, a camisole, half slips, and socks. Make a nightshirt or nightgown for bedtime, or make both.

Nightshirt

Nightgown

Tights, Camisole, Panties, Half Slips, and Socks

Panties

Like commercial mini doll panties, the elastic on these panties will be on the right side of the fabric.

You will need: a small piece of one-way stretch knit, such as nylon tricot or T-shirt knit, tear-away stabilizer, and ⅛" (3 mm) wide elastic.

Cutting and Marking

- Cut out one pair of panties.
- Cut a rectangle of stabilizer to go under the panties.
- Mark the notches.

Sewing Elastic to Leg and Waist Openings

- You will zigzag the elastic to the leg openings without pulling the elastic.
- Lay the panties right side up on top of the stabilizer.
- Lay elastic on the right side of one pantie leg opening.
- Anchor the elastic by sewing it down at one end of the leg opening.
- Use a wide zigzag to sew on either side of the elastic. Do not catch the elastic with the needle.
- When you have finished zigzagging, secure the second end of the elastic and cut off excess elastic.
- Cut away the stabilizer.
- Lay the panties back on the stabilizer and sew elastic on top of the other leg opening.
- Cut away the stabilizer.
- You will zigzag the elastic to the waist opening and pull the elastic to fit the doll's waist.
- Lay the panties right side up on top the stabilizer.
- Lay elastic on the right side of the panties at the waist edge.
- Anchor the elastic by sewing it down at one end of the waist.
- Use a wide zigzag to sew on either side of the elastic. Do not catch the elastic with the needle.

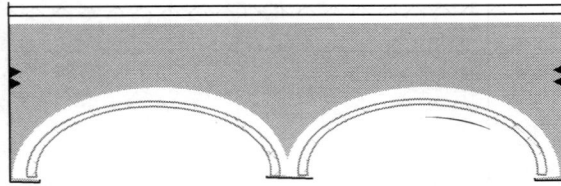

- Pull the elastic through the zigzagging without stretching the elastic until the waist measures about 4" (10 cm).
- Check the fit around the doll's waist.
- Secure the second end of the elastic by sewing it down and cut off excess elastic.

Finishing

- With right sides together match the notches.
- Place the panties back on the stabilizer and sew the center back together with a zigzag stitch.

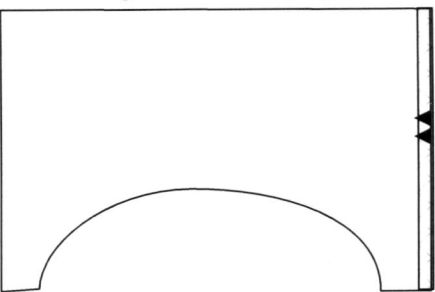

- Fold panties so that the center front and center back are touching.
- Sew the crotch using a zigzag seam.

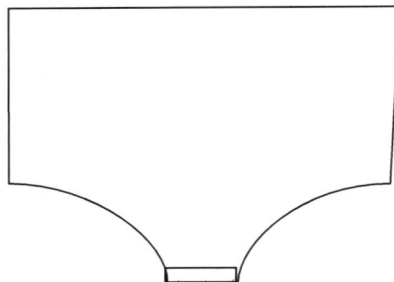

- Turn right side out.

Camisole

You will need: a small piece of one-way stretch knit, such as nylon tricot or T-shirt knit, ¼" (6 mm) wide lace edging, ⅛" (3 mm) ribbon, hook and loop tape, and optional small appliques.

Cutting and Marking

- Cut out camisole.
- Mark the A and B dots on the wrong side of the fabric.

Applying Lace

- Lay a strip of lace on the right side of the fabric at the top of the camisole. The heading of the lace should be touching the raw edge at the top of the camisole. The edge of the lace should be inside the camisole.
- Use a narrow zigzag seam. Sew lace without gathering around the top of the camisole.
- Lay a strip of lace on the right side of the fabric at the bottom of the camisole. The heading of the lace should be touching the raw edge at the bottom of the camisole. The edge of the lace should be inside the camisole.
- Use a narrow zigzag seam to sew lace edging to the bottom of the camisole.

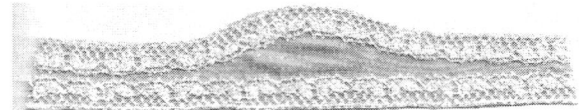

Adding Hook and Loop Tape to the Back

- Press under ½" (12 mm) of fabric on each side of the center back. Try on doll. The openings should come together at the center back.
- Sew hook and loop tape to the back of the camisole. (**Tips** p **95**)

Adding Straps

- Cut two 2½" (6 cm) lengths of ribbon.
- On the inside of the garment hand sew each piece of ribbon to the front of the garment where the A dots have been marked.
- Pin the ribbon lengths to the back of the garment where the B dots have been marked. Leave about 1" (2.5 cm) of ribbon between the A and B dots to serve as shoulder straps.

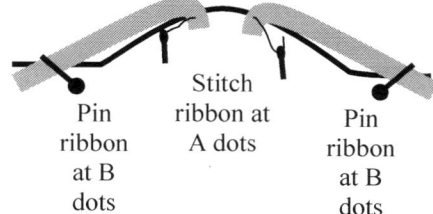

- Try the garment on the doll and adjust the straps.
- Hand sew the pinned ribbon lengths to the back of the garment.

Extras

- Sew an applique on front of camisole if desired. (**Tips p. 95**)

Tights

Like the doll panties, the elastic will be on the right side of the tights fabric.

You will need: a small piece of two way stretch knit. (You can use a piece of fabric cut from an old pair of tights.) You will also need tear-away stabilizer, seam sealant, and ⅛" (3 mm) wide elastic.

Cutting and Marking

- Cut two tights pieces from knit fabric.
- Mark the notches.

Preparing and Sewing the Center Front

- Right sides together, place the two fabric pieces together on a square of tear away stabilizer.
- Baste and then zigzag the center fronts.

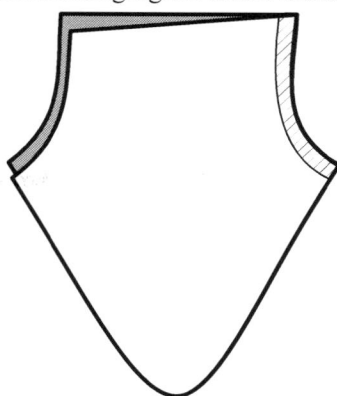

- Carefully trim away the stabilizer on both sides of the stitching.

Sewing Elastic to the Waist

- Open the tights up.
- Lay the *wrong* side of the tights touching the stabilizer and the right side of the tights facing up.
- Lay elastic on the right side of the tights at the waist edge.
- Anchor the elastic by sewing it down at one end of the waist.
- Use a wide zigzag to sew on either side of the elastic. Do not catch the elastic with the needle.

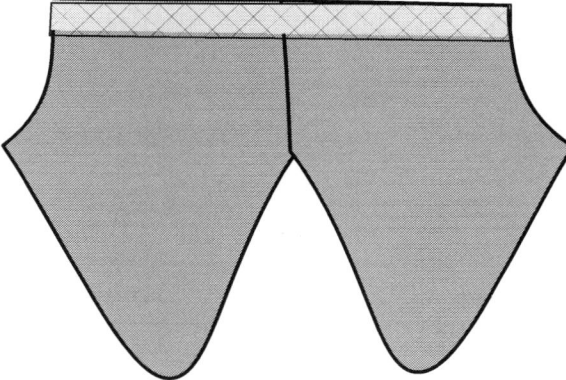

- When you have finished zigzagging, measure the waist.
- The waist should measure 4" (10 cm). If you have not stretched the waist fabric while sewing on the elastic, you will not need to pull the elastic. The waist will be the correct size.
- Secure the second end of the elastic by sewing it down and cut off excess elastic.
- Cut away the stabilizer.

Preparing and Sewing the Center Back

- Refold the tights so that they are right sides together. The waist elastic will be on the inside of the tights until construction is complete.
- Place the tights back on a square of tear away stabilizer.

- Baste and then zigzag the center backs.

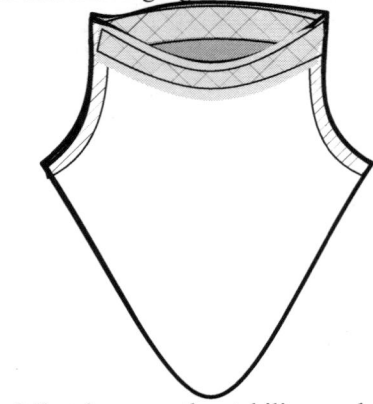

- Carefully trim away the stabilizer on both sides of the stitching.

Preparing and Sewing the Leg Seam

- Open up the tights and bring the sides of each leg together.
- Baste the leg seams to the stabilizer and the zigzag the leg seam.

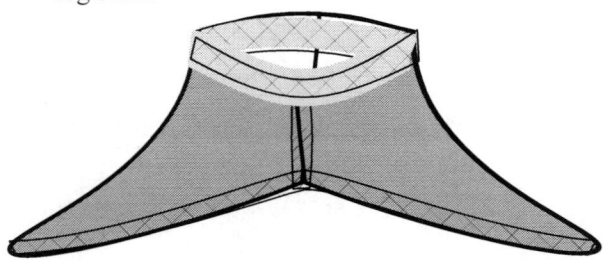

Finishing

- Carefully trim away the stabilizer.
- Turn right side out.

Half Slips

Like the doll panties and tights, the elastic will be on the right side of the half slip.

For the short slip you will need: a twenty inch (50 cm) length of ½" (1.3 cm) wide lace, and ⅛" (3 mm) wide elastic. For a long slip you will need thirty-two inches (80 cm) of lace.

Cutting

For the short slip divide the lace into an 8" (20 cm) piece of lace and a 12" (30 cm) piece of lace. For a long slip divide the lace into an 8" (20 cm) piece of lace and two 12" (30 cm) pieces of lace.

Preparing the Lace

- For a long slip zigzag the two longer pieces of lace together and continue as you would sew a short slip.
- Pull a thread in the heading of the 12" (30 cm) lace until it measures 8" (20 cm).

- If the chosen lace does not have a heading thread, sew a gathering thread in the heading by hand or machine and pull the thread until it measures 8" (20 cm).

Sewing the Lace Pieces Together

- Lay the bottom edge of the 8" (20 cm) lace piece on top of the gathered edge of the second lace piece. The pieces should only overlap about a sixteenth of an inch (2 mm).
- Use a narrow zigzag stitch to join the two pieces together.

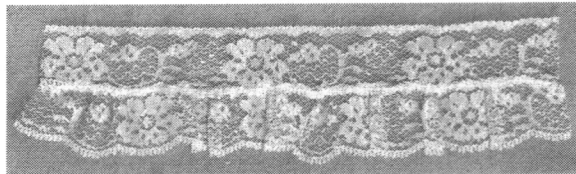

Sewing Elastic to the Waist

- Lay elastic on the right side of the slip at the waist edge.
- Anchor the elastic by sewing it down at one end of the waist.
- Use a wide zigzag to sew on either side of the elastic. Do not catch the elastic with the needle.

- Pull the elastic through the zigzagged thread to about 4" (10 cm) without stretching the elastic.
- Check the fit around the doll's waist.
- Secure the second end of the elastic by sewing it down and cut off excess elastic.

Finishing

- Right sides together, sew the center back of the slip together.
- Turn right side out.

Nightshirt

You will need: T-shirt knit in the color of your choice, matching or contrasting ribbing (sometimes T-shirt knit works as a ribbing substitute), optional applique and matching thread.

Cutting and Marking

- Cut one front on fold, two backs, two sleeves, and one neck ribbing.
- Check arrows before cutting to make certain the patterns are aligned correctly with the fabric's stretch.
- Mark the notches and dots.

Sewing the Shoulder Seams

- Right sides together match single notches at the shoulder seams.
- Use a ⅛" (3 mm) wide zigzag to sew the shoulder seams.

Attaching the Neckband

- Fold the ribbing in half with wrong sides together.
- Press.
- Place the folded ribbing on the right side of the nightshirt with the raw edges next to the neck's raw edge.
- Do not fold the back closing to the inside until the ribbing has been sown to the neck. Start applying ribbing at the raw edge of the shirt back.
- Stretch the ribbing with gentle consistent pressure while zigzagging it to the neck. The ribbing must be stretched to fit the neck.

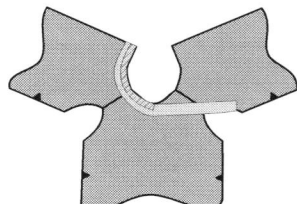

Setting in Sleeves

- Press the sleeve hem ¼" (6 mm) to the inside of the fabric and zigzag.
- Match the dot at the top of the sleeve to the shoulder seam.
- Right sides together, pin and then hand baste the sleeve into the arm opening.

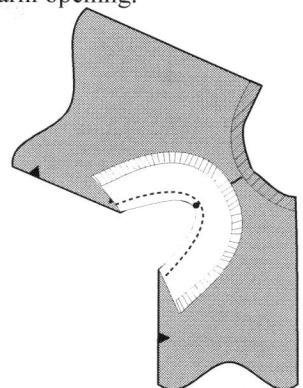

- Zigzag the sleeve to the shirt.

Finishing the Night shirt

- Match the single notches and dots on the shirt sides and zigzag across the sleeves and down the sides stopping at the dots.
- Starting at the dots, press the nightshirt hem and zigzag.

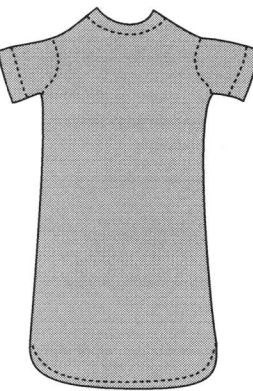

- Press both back openings ½" (12 mm) under.
- Apply hook and loop tape. (**Tips** p. 95)
- Turn under the raw edge at the bottom of the T-shirt ½" (12 cm) and zigzag the hem.
- You may add an optional applique, if you like. (**Tips** p. 95)

Nightgown or Smock

You will need: scraps of soft cotton fabric with soft colors or small prints (you may use cotton flannel for the gown if you like), matching thread, optional narrow ribbon, and hook and loop tape.

Cutting and Marking

- Cut one smock or gown front on the fold and two backs.
- Mark the notches.

Sewing Shoulder/Sleeve Seams

- Match the single notches at the the shoulder seam/sleeve top.
- Sew shoulder seams and finish the seams. If you are finishing the seam with zigzagging or serging, finish both sides of the seam together. The seam will not be pressed open.
- Press the finished seam to the back of the garment.
- Finish the raw edges of sleeves, neck, and back closings.
- Press the back closings ½" (12 mm) to the inside and then the neck edge ¼" (6 mm) to the inside. The top edges of the back opening will be folded to the inside along with the rest of the neck edge.

Hand Gathering the Neck

- Start at the center back. Hand gather the neck. Sew near the neck opening and catch all the fabric layers that have been pressed to the inside of the garment. Gather the neck to 3⅜" (9 cm).

Sewing Elastic Casing in Sleeves

- To make each sleeve casing press the finished casing edge ½" (12 mm) to the inside. Topstitch ⅜" (9 mm) from the edge.

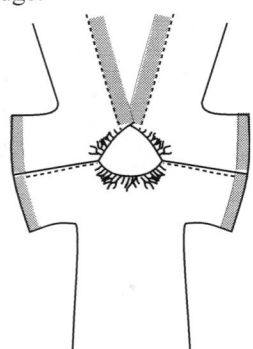

- Insert elastic into the casing and anchor one end of the elastic by sewing it down at one casing opening.
- Gather the casing fabric over the elastic to about 1⅞" (5 cm). Do not stretch the elastic
- Check the fit around the wrist on the doll.
- Secure the second side of the elastic to the second casing opening by sewing through it and the casing several times. Cut off the excess elastic.

Sides, Back, and Hem

- Fold right sides together at the shoulder seams and match the double notches at the garment's sides.
- Sew across the bottom of each sleeve and down the garment's side.

- Finish the seams.

- Either garment opens all the way down the back. Close the back with hook and loop tape. (**Tips** p **95**)
- Finish the raw edge of the hem.
- Press a ½" (12 mm) hem in the gown, or a ¼" (6 mm) hem in the top and topstitch or whip in the hem.
- Add a bow at the neckline, if you wish.

Sock

You will need: a small piece of two way stretch knit. You can use a sock, if you like.

Cutting and Marking

- Cut socks on the fold.
- If you are using a sock for your source of knit fabric, you can place the top of the sock pattern at the finished top of your sock. Then you can skip the *Finishing the Top* section of the instructions and go straight to *Sewing the Sock*.

Finishing the Top

- To finish the top, open the folded fabric and turn ⅛" (3 mm) of fabric to the wrong side of the sock and zigzag.

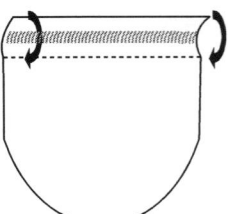

Sewing the Sock

- Refold each sock so that the right sides are together.
- Use a narrow zigzag stitch to sew from the top of the sock down the side and around the foot to the toe.
- Turn the sock right side out.

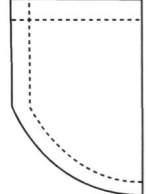

Undies, Night Shirt, and Socks

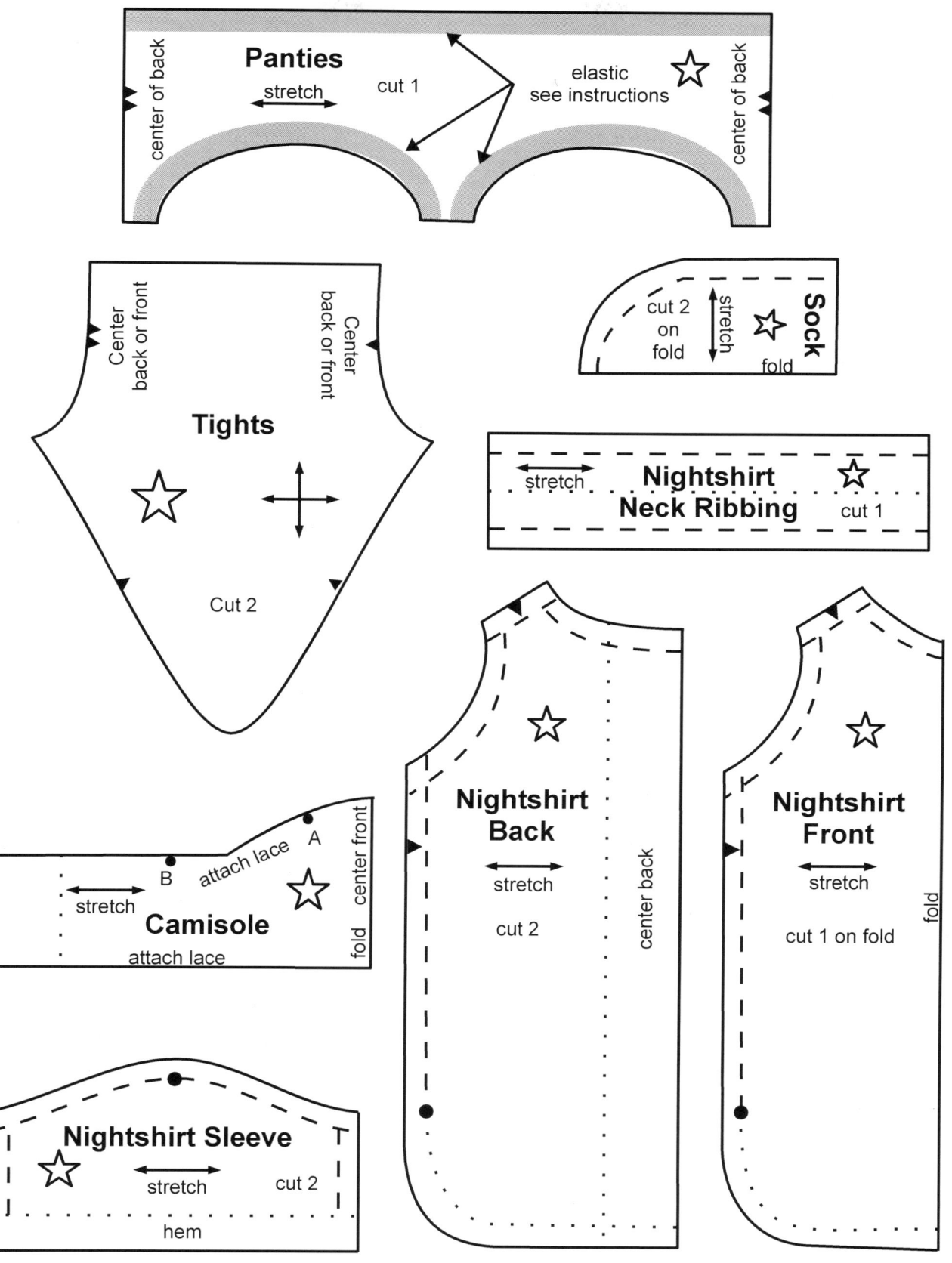

Nightgown

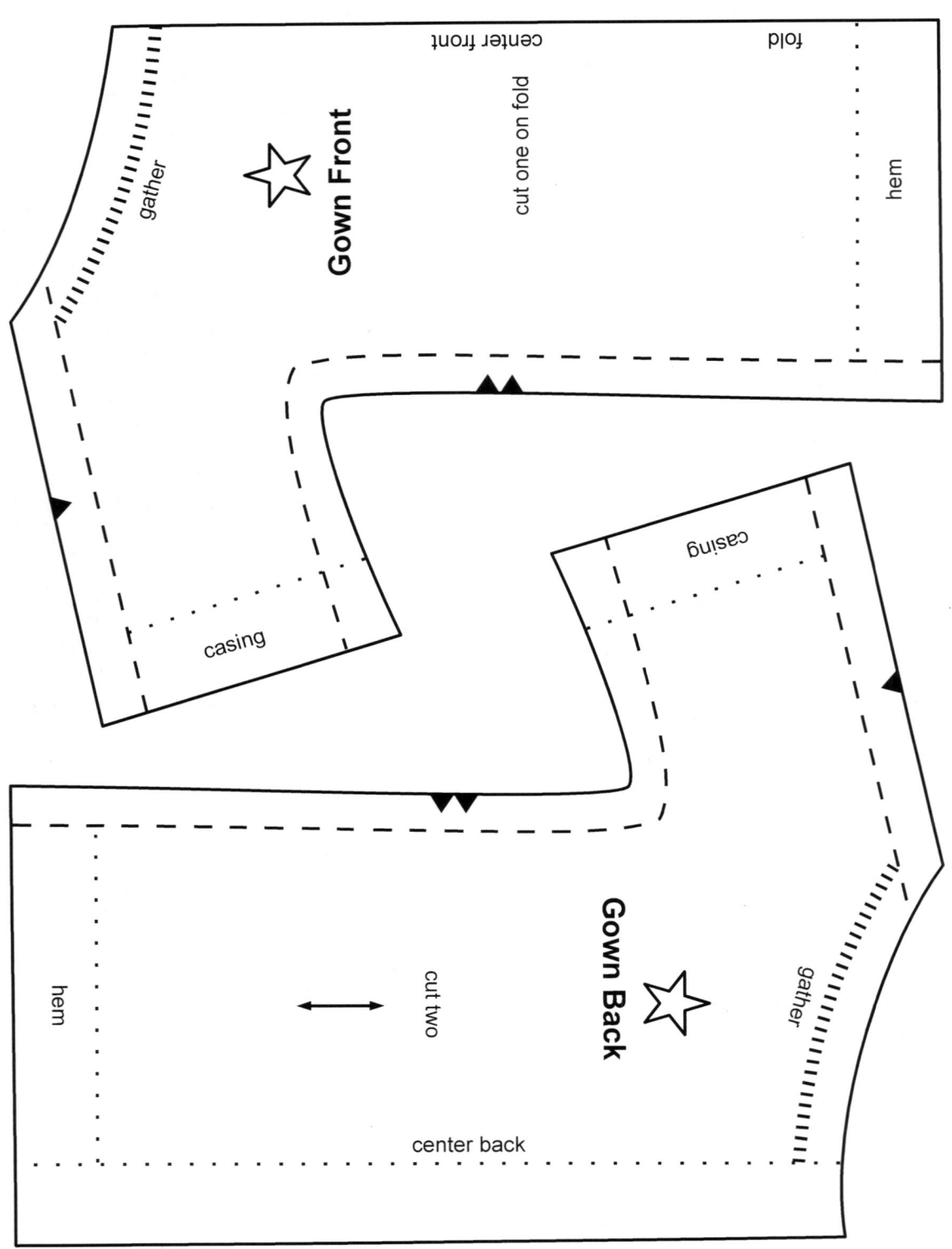

Sewing for Mini Dolls
www.sherralynsdolls.com

Separates

A mini doll can have a typical kid's wardrobe with all the mix and match choices from this chapter. Make long pants or shorts. Use jean or khaki fabric for casual pants, if you like. Make an A-line or two tiered skirt. Patterns for adding optional pockets to the pants and A-line skirt are included. Tops include a T-shirt, pull-over sweater, smock, and summer top. A short jacket can be used with the T-shirt and summer top from this chapter and the A-line dress and sundress from the next chapter.

Shorts and T-shirt

Sweater and Jeans

A-line Skirt and T-Shirt

Smock and Two Tiered Skirt

Summer Top, Two Tiered Skirt, and Jacket

Pants

You will need: cotton broadcloth in the color or design of your choice, blue or khaki colored broadcloth for jeans or khakis, matching thread, optional orange thread for jeans topstitching, and sewing glue stick for optional pockets.

Cutting and Marking

- Cut two of the jeans or shorts pattern.
- Mark the notches.

Applying Patch Pockets (optional)

- If you do not wish to apply pockets, go to the section marked *Finishing the Pants Leg Bottoms*.
- This method of applying pockets makes it easier to produce pockets of a consistent size and shape.
- Fold a small scrap of pants fabric in half, right sides together.
- Draw two pockets on the folded fabric by tracing around the pocket template.
- You can also use freezer paper to mark the pocket outline. (**Tips p. 92**)
- Sew on the traced lines or around the freezer paper.
- Leave the top of the pocket open.
- Cut out pockets using a ⅛" (3 mm) seam allowance. Note the clipped corners.

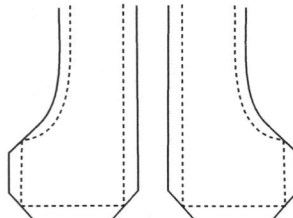

- Turn pockets right side out through the top opening and press.
- Topstitch the curved area that will be left open when the pocket is sewn to the pants. Use gold or orange thread for the blue jeans if you like.

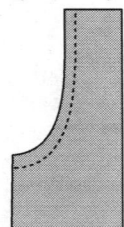

- Mark the pocket placement on the right side of the pants fabric with air soluble pen.
- Place pockets over placement markings.
- Pin in place or use sewing glue stick.

- Topstitch around the three straight areas of the pocket. Leave the previously stitched curved area open. Use orange or gold thread for blue jeans if you like.

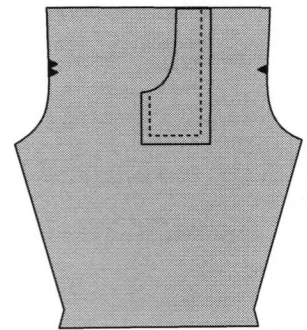

Finishing the Pants Leg Bottoms

- Finish the raw edges at the bottom of each leg.
- Turn ¼" (6 mm) to the inside at each leg bottom.
- Topstitch and press.

Making the Casing and Inserting Elastic

- Match the single notches and sew the center fronts together.
- Finish the seam. Finish the two raw edges together so that they can be pressed in one direction. If the seam is pressed open, it will be difficult to insert the elastic once the casing is constructed.

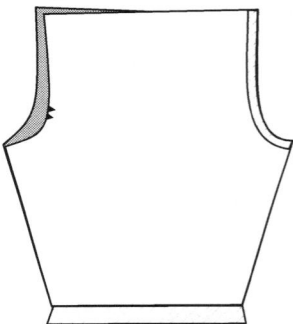

- Finish the raw edge at the top of the waist. Press the fabric in ½" (12 mm) to the inside.
- Topstitch ¼" to ⅜" (6 to 9 mm) from the folded edge at the top of the pants.
- Insert the elastic into the casing. Sew one end of the elastic along the raw edge of the casing.
- Gather the casing fabric to 4" (10 cm) over the elastic without stretching the elastic.

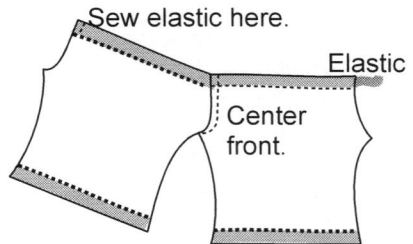

- Try the pants around the doll's waist and adjust if necessary. Secure the second side of the elastic by sewing across it through the casing several times. Cut off the excess elastic.

Finishing the Pants

- Match the double notches and sew center backs together.

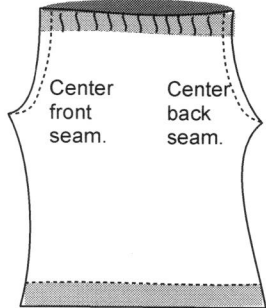

- Bring the center fronts and center backs together and sew the inside leg seams.

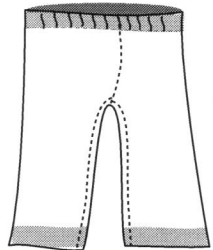

- Turn right side out.

Skirt

You will need: cotton broadcloth in the color or design of your choice, blue or khaki colored broadcloth for jeans or khakis skirt, matching thread, optional orange thread for jeans skirt topstitching, and sewing glue stick for optional pockets.

Cutting and Marking

- Cut one front and one back skirt from the skirt pattern.
- Mark the notches.

Applying Patch Pockets

- If you do not wish to apply pockets, go to the section marked *Making the Casing and Inserting Elastic*.
- This method of applying pockets makes it easier to produce pockets of a consistent size and shape.
- Fold a small scrap of skirt fabric in half right sides together.
- Draw two skirt pockets on the folded fabric by tracing around the skirt pocket template.
- You can also use freezer paper to mark the pocket outline. (**Tips** p. 92)
- Sew on the traced lines or around the freezer paper.
- Leave the top and sides of the pocket open.

- Cut out pockets using a ⅛" (3 mm) seam allowance.

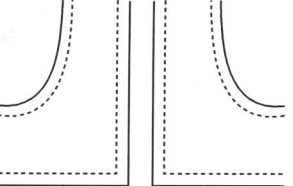

- Turn pockets right side out.
- Topstitch the curved area that will be left open when the pocket is sewn to the skirt. Use gold or orange thread for a blue jean skirt if you like.

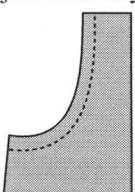

- Mark the pocket placement on the right side of the skirt fabric with air soluble pen. Mark the pockets on only one cut skirt piece. The pockets will define the skirt front.
- Place pockets over placement markings.
- Pin in place or use sewing glue stick.
- Topstitch around the two straight areas that will not be caught in the seam. Use orange or gold thread for a blue jean skirt, if you like.

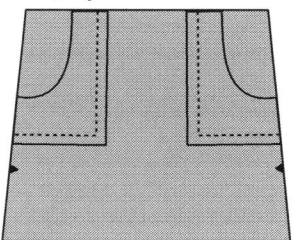

Making the Casing and Inserting Elastic

- Sew one side of the skirt front to the skirt back matching the single notches.
- Finish the seam. Finish the two raw edges together, so that they can be pressed in one direction. If the seam is pressed open, it will be difficult to insert the elastic once the casing is constructed.
- To make the casing, open the skirt up and finish the raw edge at the top of the waist.
- Press the fabric in ½" (12 mm) to the inside.
- Top stitch ¼" to ⅜" (6 to 9 mm) from the folded edge at the top of the skirt.
- Insert the elastic into the casing. Sew one end of the elastic along a raw edge of the casing opening.

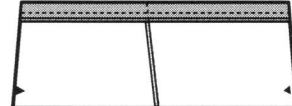

- Gather the casing fabric to 4" (10 cm) over the elastic without stretching the elastic.

17

- Try the skirt around the doll's waist and adjust if necessary. Secure the second side of the elastic and cut off the excess.

Finishing the Skirt

- Finish the raw edge at the bottom of the skirt.
- If you would like to topstitch the hem, press the hem ½" (12 mm) to the inside and topstitch.
- Sew the second side of skirt front to skirt back, matching single notches.
- Finish the seam.
- If you plan to slip-stitch the hem, sew the second side of skirt front to skirt back before hemming.
- Press the hem ½" (12 mm) to the inside and slip-stitch.
- Turn right side out.

Two Tier Skirt

You will need: scraps of soft cotton fabric with soft colors or small prints, matching thread, and ⅛" (3 mm) elastic.

Cutting and Marking

- Cut one skirt top tier and one skirt bottom tier on the fold.
- Mark notches and the center front.

Joining the Gathered Tier to the Top Tier

- Run two parallel lines of gathering stitches where indicated on skirt bottom tier.

- Pull up the gathering stitches to match the skirt top tier. Match the notches and the center front.
- Pin or baste the two tiers and sew them together.

- Finish the seam.

Sewing Elastic Casing in Skirt

- Finish the the raw edges at the top and bottom of the skirt.
- To make a casing at the skirt's waist press the finished casing edge ½" (12 mm) to the inside.
- Topstitch ¼" to ⅜" (6 to 9 mm) from the edge.

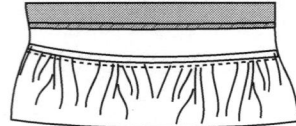

- Insert elastic into the casing and anchor one end of the elastic by sewing it down at one casing opening.
- Gather the casing fabric over the elastic to about 4" (10 cm). Do not stretch the elastic.

- Check the fit on the doll's waist and secure the second side of the elastic by sewing through it and the casing several times.

Finishing the Skirt

- Sew the back closing and finish the seam.
- Press the hem ¼" (6 mm) to the inside. Slip-stitch or topstitch the hem.

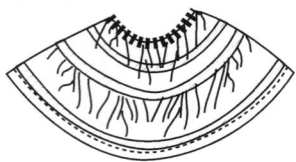

T-shirt

You will need: T-shirt knit in color of your choice, matching or contrasting ribbing (sometimes T-shirt knit works as a ribbing substitute), optional applique, and matching thread.

Cutting and Marking

- Cut one front on fold, two backs, two sleeves, and one neck ribbing. The neck ribbing should be cut from real ribbing, if you have it. Sometimes, when the knit is stretchy enough, T-shirt knit works as a ribbing substitute.
- Check arrows before cutting to make certain the patterns are aligned correctly with the fabric's stretch.
- Mark the dot on the sleeves.

Sewing Knit with Zigzag Seams

- Use zigzag stitches to join the T-shirt. I have not had success using a serger on these small T-shirts.
- Use a zigzag stitch slightly more narrow than the seam allowance to join knits. Set the zigzags to be fairly close together, but not as close as a satin stitch.
- Note that the seam allowance is only ⅛" (3 mm).
- If your zigzag is less than ⅛" (3 mm) wide, you may trim the seam.

Sewing the Shoulder Seams

- Right sides together match single notches at shoulder seams.
- Sew shoulder seams.

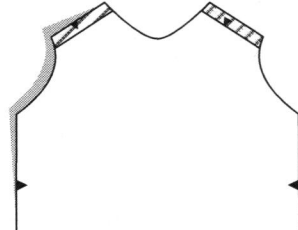

Attaching the Neckband

- Fold the ribbing in half with wrong sides together.
- Press.

- Place the folded ribbing on the right side of the shirt with the raw edges next to the neck raw edge.
- Do not fold the back closing to the inside until the ribbing has been sown to the neck. Start applying ribbing at the raw edge of the shirt back.
- Stretch the ribbing with gentle consistent pressure while zigzagging it to the neck. The ribbing must be stretched to fit the neck.

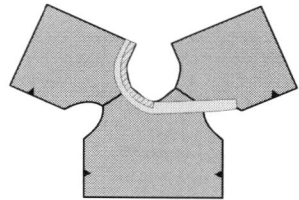

Setting in the Sleeves

- Press the sleeve hem ¼" (6 mm) to the inside of the fabric.
- Zigzag.
- Match the dot at the top of the sleeve to the shoulder seam.
- Right sides together, pin and then hand baste the sleeve into the arm opening.

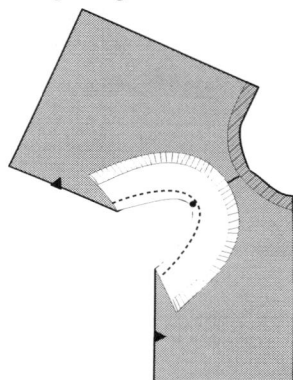

- Zigzag the sleeve to the shirt.

Finishing the T-shirt

- Match the single notches on the shirt sides and zigzag across the sleeves and down the sides.
- Press the T-shirt hem and zigzag.

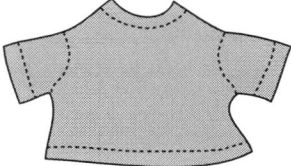

- Press both back openings ½" (12 mm) under.
- Apply hook and loop tape. (**Tips** p. **95**)
- Turn under the raw edge at the bottom of the T-shirt ½" (12 cm) and zigzag the hem.
- Add optional applique. (**Tips** p. **95**)

Smock Top

Use directions for nightgown p. 11 to make smock top.

Summer Top

Use directions for sundress p. 31 to make summer top.

Puller-Over Sweater

You will need: One pair of baby socks whose top opening measures 2¼" (6 cm), a small amount of tear away stabilizer, and seam sealant.

Measuring and Cutting

- Starting at the top of the first sock, measure down 2¼" (6 cm) and cut across the sock. This piece of the sock will be the sweater body. On the second sock measure down 1¾" (4 cm) and cut across the sock. You will make the sleeves with this piece.

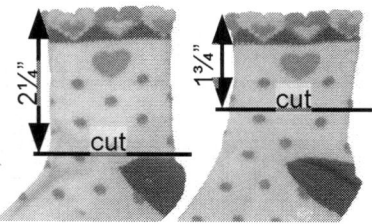

- Cut two 1" (2.5 cm) sleeve slits at the top sides of the sweater body. Starting at the sock top, cut the sweater sleeve piece in half.

- You now have a sweater body with two sleeve slits, a left sleeve, and a right sleeve.

- Put seam sealant all the way around the raw edge at the bottom of the sweater body and let it dry.

Preparing to Sew

- Lay one open sleeve on each side of the sweater body.

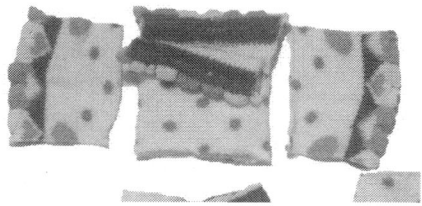

- Pivot the sleeves so that the sock top section of each sleeve is next to the sweater body. Fold down the sleeve slits on the sweater body.

- Slip the left sleeve under the sweater body. The illustration shows edge A and edge B pinned together. Before zigzagging the sleeve to the sleeve slit, you need to add tear away stabilizer and then baste.

Adding Stabilizer and Basting

- Cut a 3"x1" (8 cm x 2.5 cm) square of tear away stabilizer. Slip the stabilizer under the left sleeve and the sweater body.
- Baste edge A, edge B, and the tear away stabilizer together. The sleeve will need to be stretched slightly as you baste.

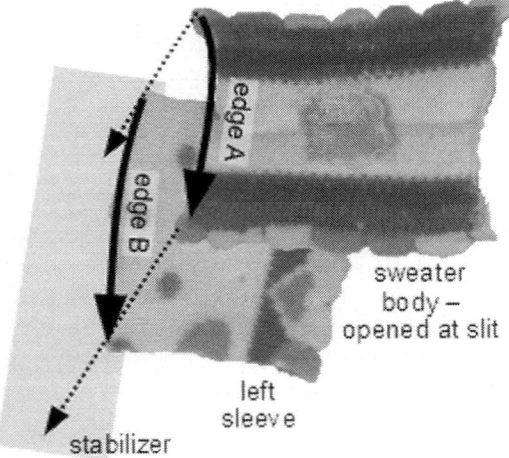

Sewing Sleeves to Sweater

- Zigzag the sleeve to the edge of the sleeve slit.

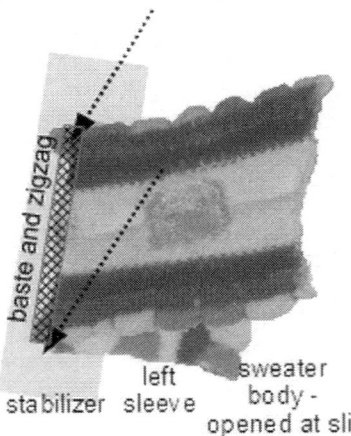

- The picture below shows the left sleeve pulled out from under the sweater body. You can see the tear away stabilizer sticking up at the seam line.

- Go back to the beginning of *Adding Stabilizer and Basting* and sew the right sleeve.
- The picture below shows both sleeves pulled out from under the sweater body. The stabilizer has not been cut away.

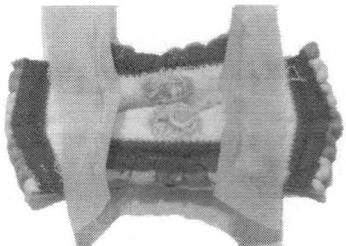

Finishing the Sweater

- If you lift up the sleeve slit with the sewn sleeves, you can see how the finished sweater will look once you have sewn the tops of the sleeves.

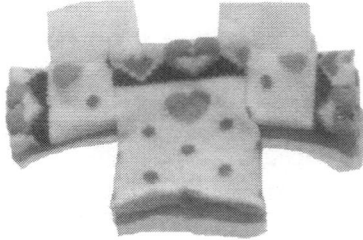

- Carefully cut the stabilizer away on each side of the stitching. Do not tear the stabilizer away, because it will stretch the knit.
- Turn the sweater wrong side out.

- Cut a 7"x1" (18 cm x 2.5 cm) strip of tear away stabilizer. Baste the tops of the sweater sleeves together and onto the tear away stabilizer.
- Zigzag across the top of each sleeve. Sew one or two zigzag stitches into the sweater body at the end of each sleeve.
- Carefully cut the stabilizer away on each side of the stitching.
- Turn the sweater right side out.

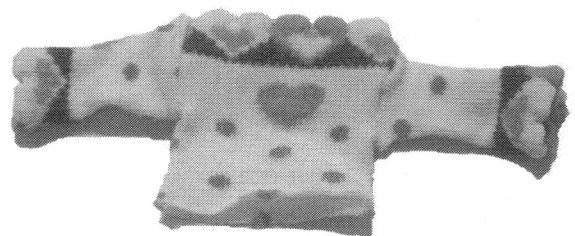

- Press seams open.
- Right sides together, pin or baste jacket to the lining.
- Sew jacket front and neck to lining and sew the bottom of jacket back to lining.

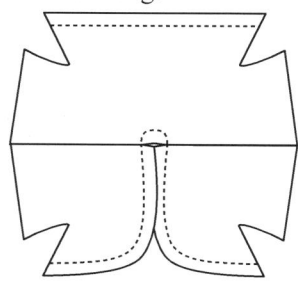

- Clip corners and curves.

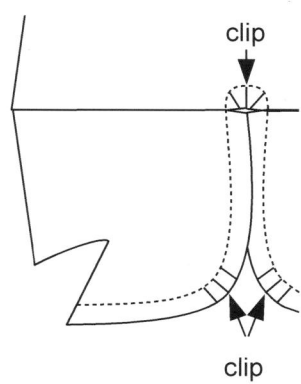

Short Jacket

A doll can wear this jacket over the T-shirt, summer top, A-line dress, or sundress.

You will need: light cotton fabric scraps in soft colors or small prints and matching thread. You may choose different fabrics for the jacket and lining.

Cutting and Marking

- Cut two fronts and two front linings.
- Cut one back and one back lining on fold.
- Mark the notches.

Lining the Jacket

- Match single notches at should/sleeve top for jacket.
- Sew jacket together at shoulder/sleeve top.

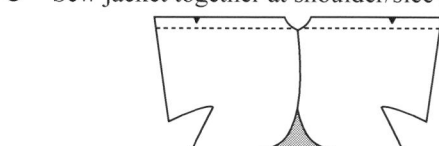

- Press seams open.
- Sew the same seams for lining.

- Turn jacket right side out through unsewn sides and sleeves.

Jacket ready for turning.

Pull first side through sleeve opening.

Continue pulling first side through opening.

Finish turning jacket.

- Press.

Finishing the Jacket

- Finish the lining and sleeve edge together as if they were a single piece of fabric.

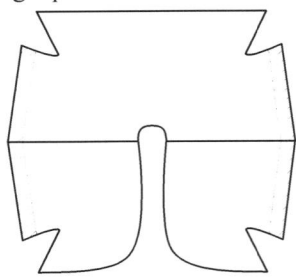

- Press the sleeve edge ¼" (6 mm) to the inside.
- Topstitch.
- Fold jacket right sides together at shoulder/sleeve top.

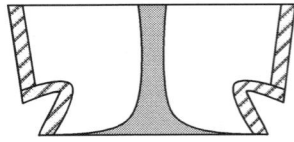

- Match double notches.
- Sew around sleeve bottoms and jacket sides.
- Finish seams. Zigzagging is the easiest method for finishing these small curves.
- Turn right side out
- Press.
- Topstitch around the outside of the jacket. (optional)

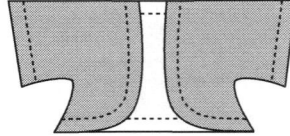

Pants and Skirt

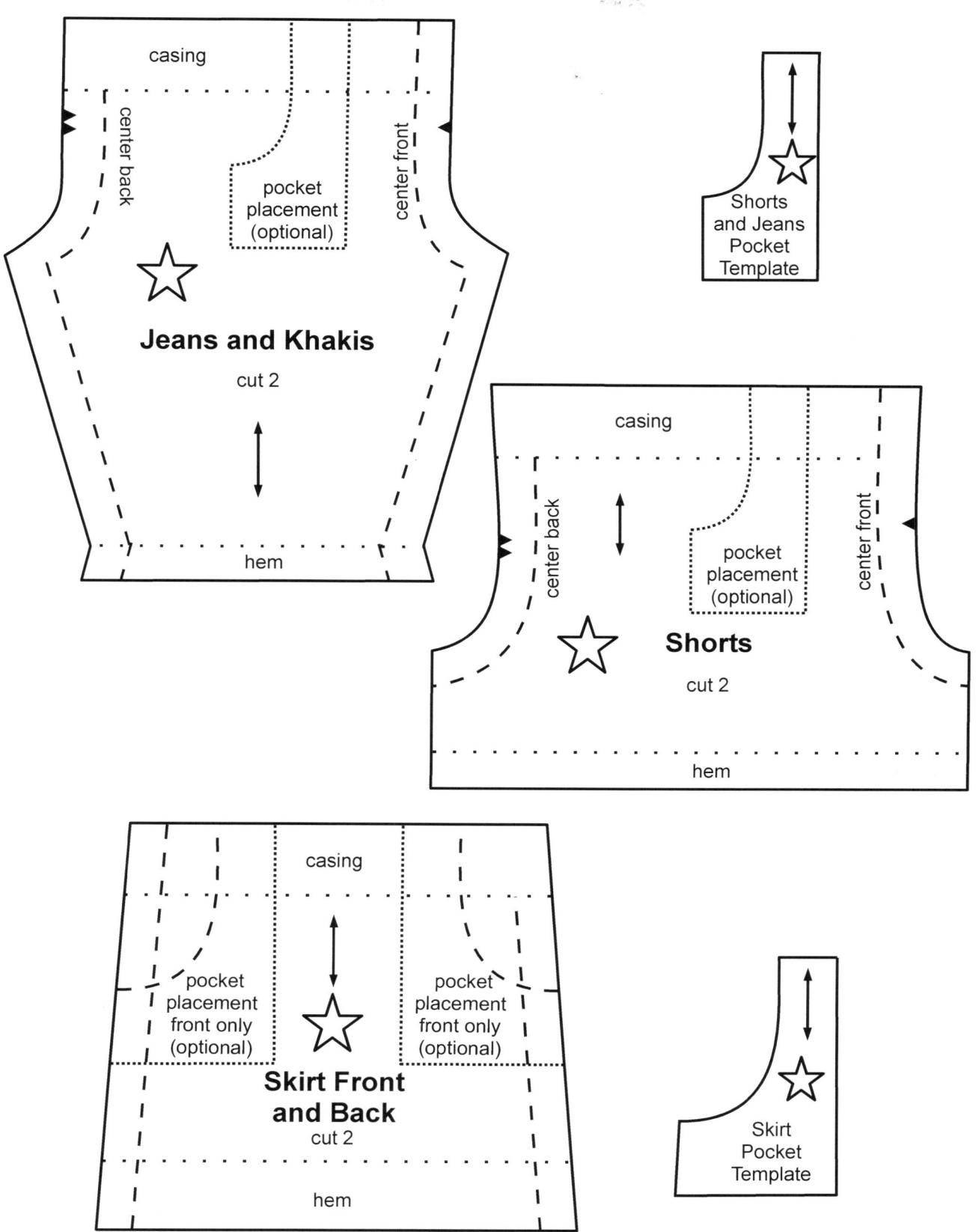

Two Tier Skirt

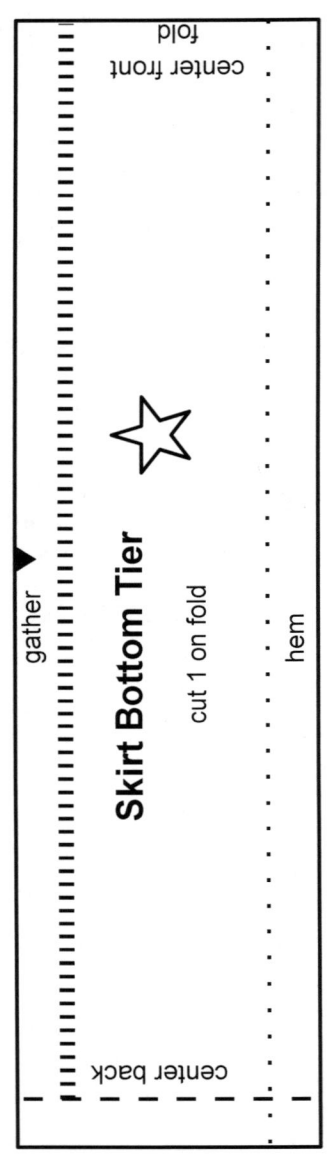
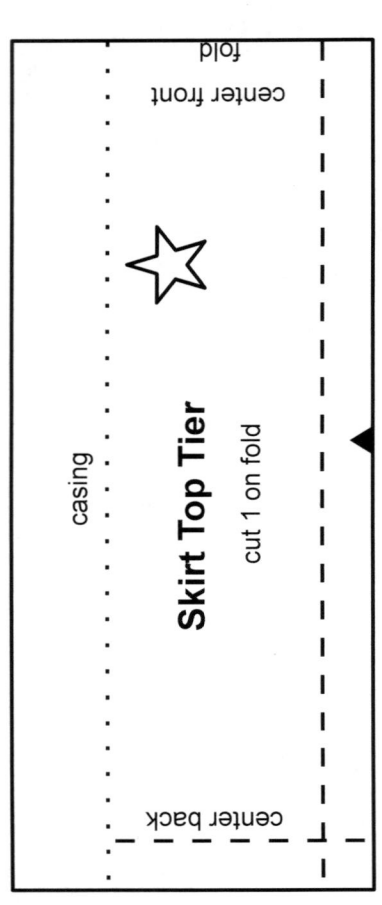

T-shirt

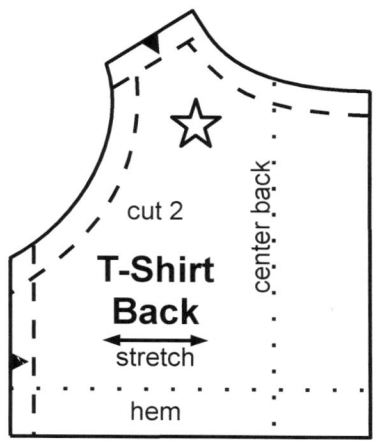
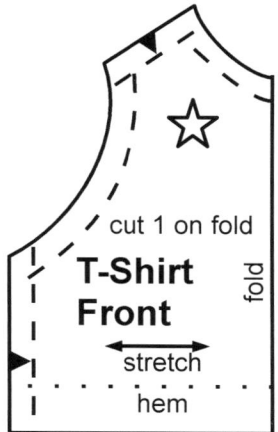
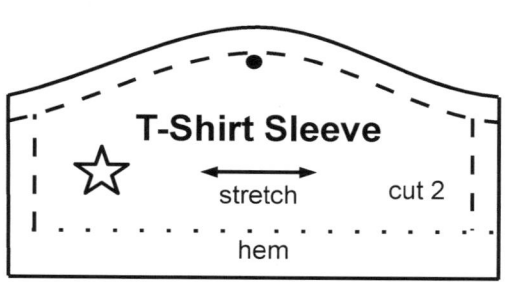

Smock Top

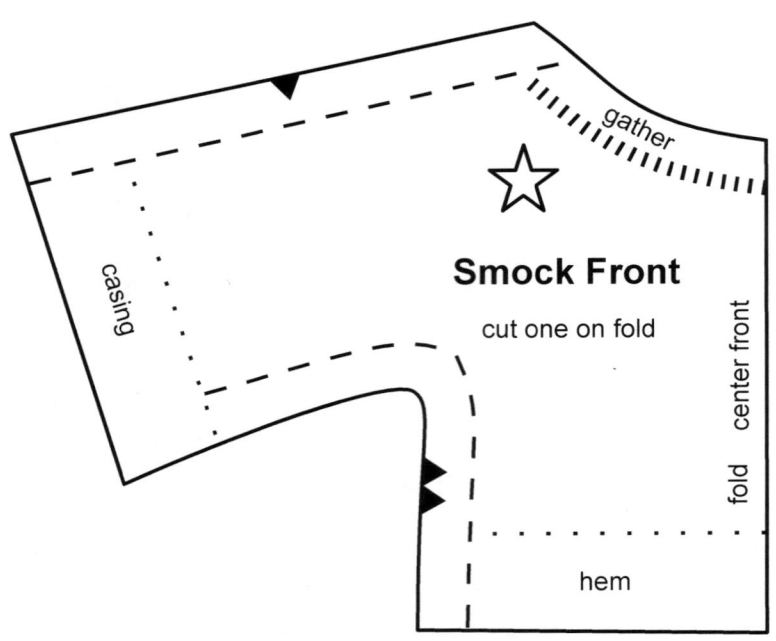

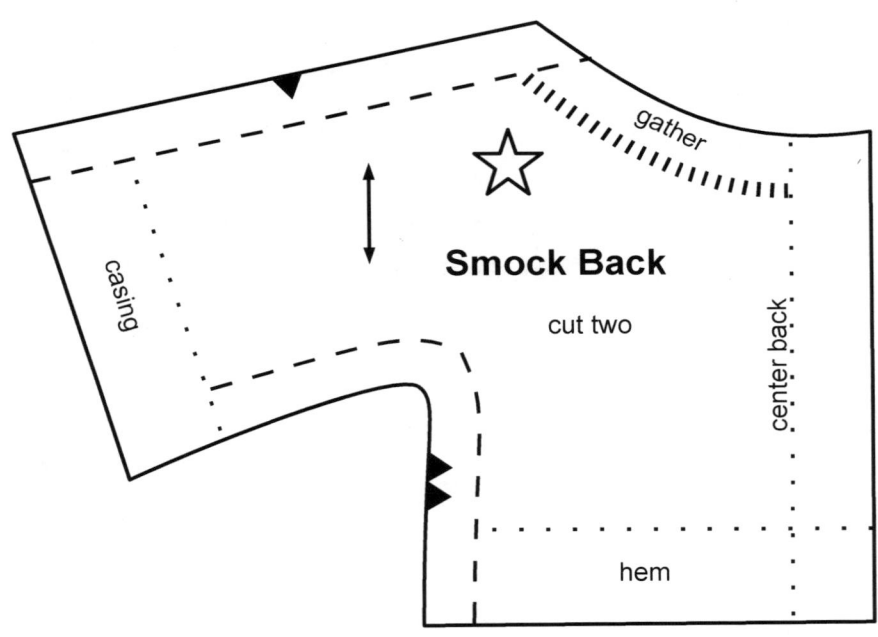

Short Jacket and Summer Top

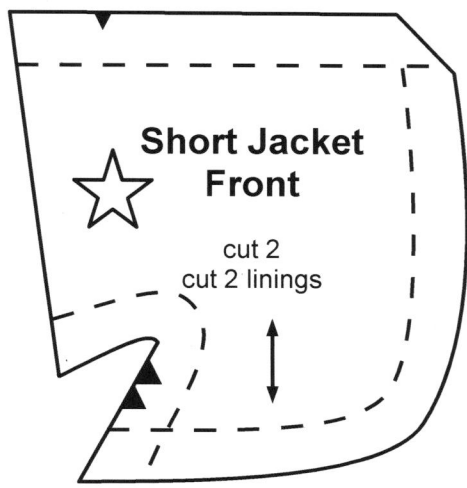
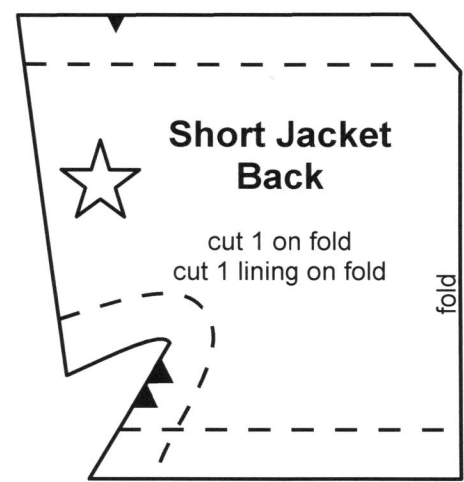
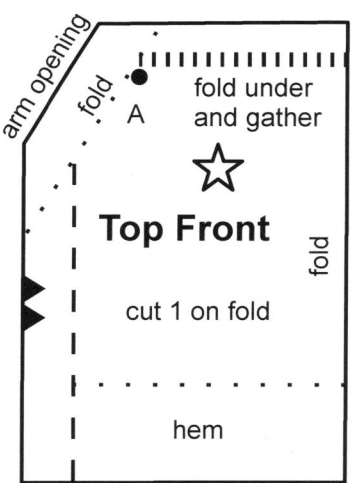
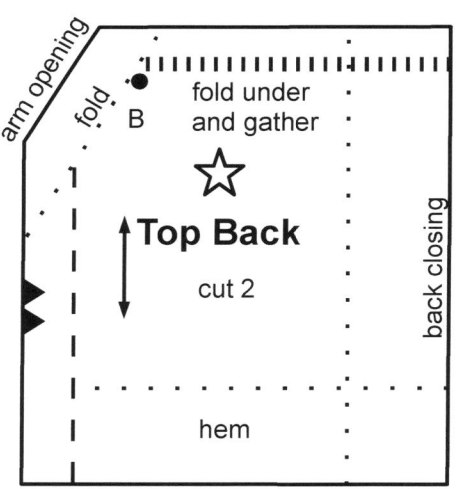

Dresses

You can use your imagination to embellish the dresses in this chapter. Add pockets or appliques to the A-line dress and sundress. Use interesting cotton prints or just your favorite colors for the A-line, sundress, or classic dress. Use silky fabric and metallic lace for a royal ballgown and add lace to the neck and hem of the classic dress or ballgown, if you like. You can add ribbon or trim to the fitted waist of these last two dresses.

Classic Dress

Princess Ballgown

A-Line Dress

Sundress

A-line Dress

You will need: light cotton fabric in soft colors or small prints, matching thread, hook and loop tape for closing back, and optional appliques.

Cutting and Marking

- Cut one front and one front facing on fold. Cut two backs and two back facings.
- Mark the notches.

Applying Facing

- Match the single notches. Sew dress front to dress backs at shoulders.
- Press seams open.
- Match the single notches. Sew facing front to facing back at shoulders.
- Press seams open.
- Finish bottom of front and back facings.
- Right sides together, lay facing on the dress matching neck, armholes, and back openings.
- Sew all the way around the neck and then around each armhole.

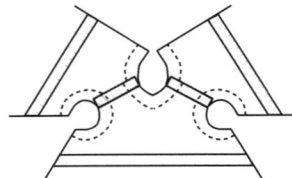

- Trim the seam to ⅛" (3 mm).
- Turn the dress right side out by pulling the facing through the space at each shoulder between the neck and armhole. Use a hemostat.

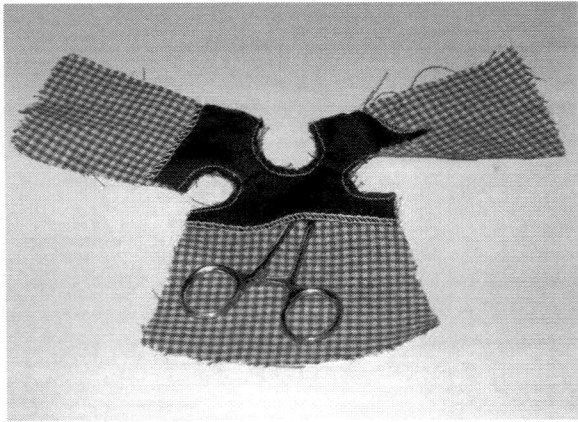

Grasp first back facing with hemostat.

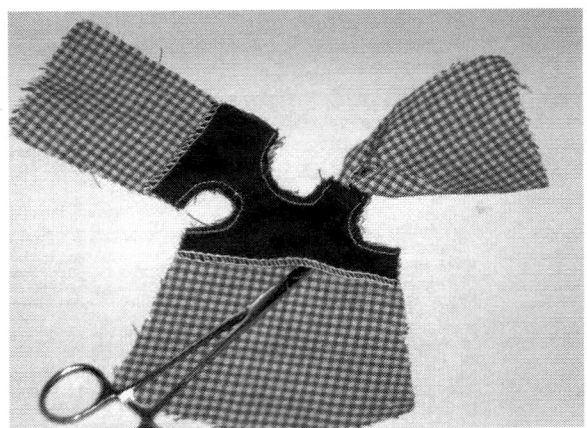

Pull facing through first shoulder space.

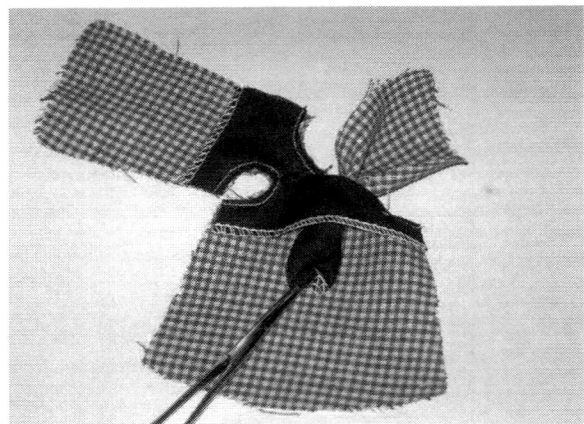

Continue pulling first facing.

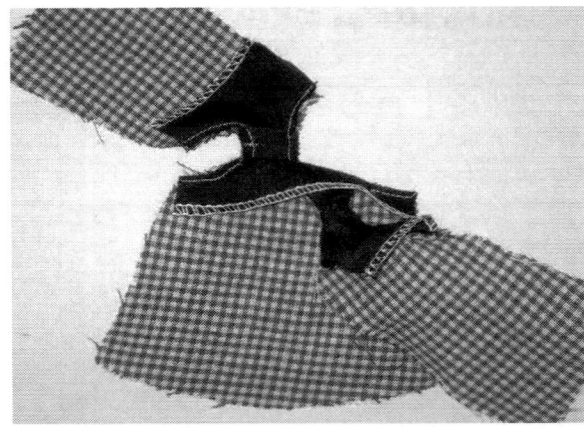

First facing pulled through.

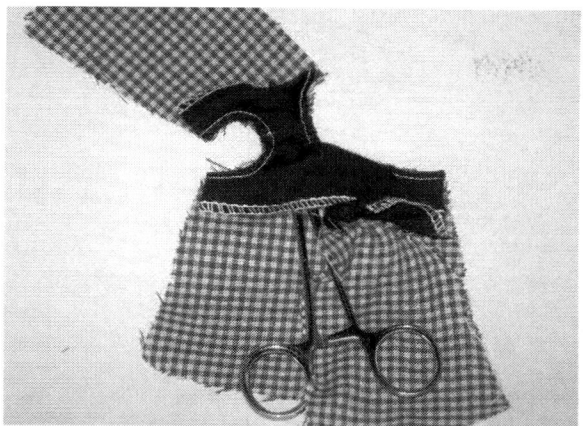

Grasp second back facing with hemostat.

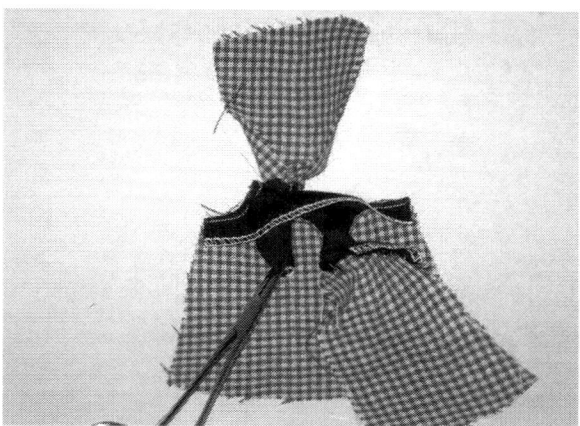

Pull second facing through.

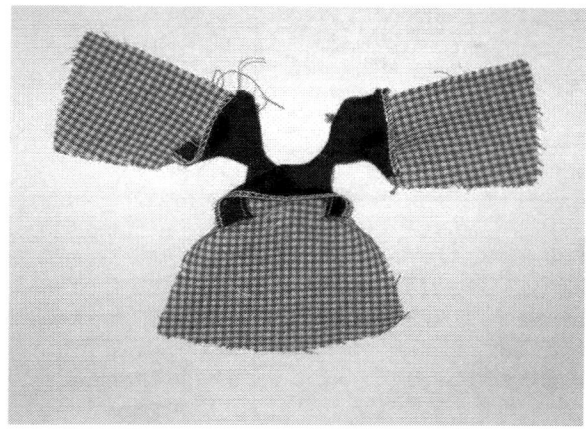

Both facings pulled through.

- Press.
- Topstitch around neck and armholes. (Optional)

Adding optional pockets

- Use the instructions in *Square and Rectangular Pockets* (**Tips p. 95**).
- Add optional pockets where indicated on the pattern.

Adding Decorations

- If you would like to add appliques to the dress use the instructions in *Appliques* (**Tips p. 95**)
- You can also add buttons or lace to the dress, if you prefer.

Sewing Side Seams

- Fold the dress at the shoulders right sides together. Match the double notches at the side seams.
- Sew side seams.
- Finish side seams.

- Turn right side out.
- Press.

Back Openings

- Finish the right facing and right back together as though they were one piece of fabric. Then finish the left back opening and left facing in the same manner.
- Press each back opening ½" (12 mm) to the inside.
- Add hook and loop tape. (**Tips p. 95**)

Hem

- Finish the bottom edge of the dress.
- Sew a gathering stitch around the finished bottom edge of the dress.
- Press a ½" (12 mm) hem in the dress.
- Pull the gathering stitch as you press, so that the hem lies flat inside the dress.
- Slip-stitch the hem.

Sundress

You will need: light cotton fabric in soft colors or small prints, matching thread, hook and loop tape for closing back, and narrow ribbon.

Cutting and Marking

- Cut one front on the fold and two backs.
- Mark the A and B dots and the double notches on the sides.

Sewing Arm Openings and Side Seams

- Finish the outside edges of the four arm openings, press ¼" (6 mm) to the inside, and topstitch.

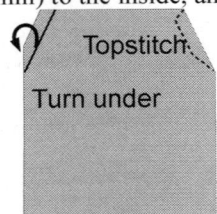

- Match the double notches and sew the sides together beginning at the bottom of the arm openings.
- Finish the seams.

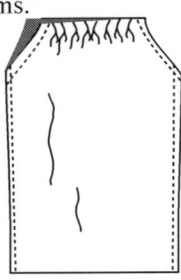

Hand Gathering the Neck

- Finish the outside edges of front and back necks, and the two sides of the back closing.
- Press the back closings ½" (12 mm) to the inside. Then press the neck edge ¼" (6 mm) to the inside. The finished top edges of the back closings will be folded to the inside along with the rest of the neck edge.
- Gather the neck front by hand. Catch the fabric layer that has been pressed to the inside. Gather the front to 1" (2.5 cm). Gather each side of the neck back by hand. Catch all the fabric layers that have been pressed to the inside of the garment including the top of the folded back closing in the gathering stitches. Gather each back piece to ½" (12 mm).

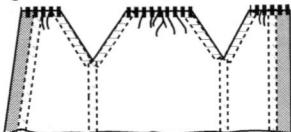

Adding Optional Pockets

- Use the instructions in *Square and Rectangular Pockets* (**Tips** p. 95).
- Add optional pockets where indicated on the pattern.

Making Ribbon Shoulder Strap

- Cut two 2½" (6.4 cm) lengths of ribbon.
- On the inside of the garment hand sew each piece of ribbon to the front of the garment where the A dots have been marked.
- Pin the ribbon lengths to the back of the garment where the B dots have been marked. Leave about 1" (2.5 cm) of ribbon between the dots.
- Try the garment on the doll.
- Check and adjust the ribbon length.

- Hand sew the ribbon at B dots.

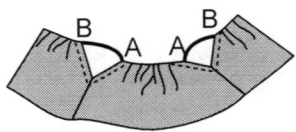

Closing the Garment

- Close the back with hook and loop tape. (**Tips p. 95**)

Hemming the Garment

- Remove the dress from the doll.
- Finish the raw edge of the hem.
- Fold and press ½" (12 mm) of fabric to the inside at hem.
- Topstitch or slip-stitch the hem.

Ballgown and Classic Dress

The ballgown and dress are made using the same steps. The ballgown is made with silkier fabric. It uses the longer skirt pattern. The ballgown can also be made with metallic laces and trims to give it the "royal" look.

You will need: scraps of silky or cotton fabric, matching thread, a twenty inch (50 cm) length of ½" to ¾" (12 to 19 mm) wide lace edging, plain or metallic rickrack or other trim for the waist (optional), and embroidery floss or metallic pearl floss for sewing rickrack (optional).

Cutting and Marking

- Cut out the bodice.
  - Cut one front on the fold and two backs, if you are finishing the neck with lace.
  - Cut two fronts on the fold and four backs, if you are facing the bodice.
- Cut two sleeves.
- Choose and cut a version of the skirt.
  - A short skirt with lace finishing the bottom
  - A short skirt with a hem at the bottom
  - A long skirt with lace finishing the bottom
- Cut one skirt on the fold.
- Mark the notches.
- Mark the dot at the top of each sleeve.
- The fold lines of the skirt and bodice front indicate the center front of the dress. Mark the center front on both pieces using a pin or air soluble pen.

Sewing Shoulder Seams

- Match the single notches at the shoulder.
- Sew shoulder seams and finish the seams.

- Press the finished seam to the back of the garment.

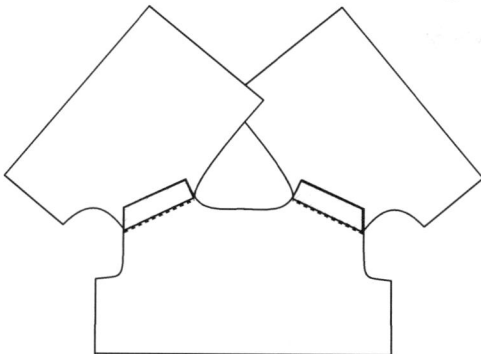

Finishing the Neck

Choose either "*Attaching Lace to the Neck,*" or "*Facing a Neck Opening.*"

Attaching Lace to the Neck

Choose this method of finishing the neck if your enjoy working with lace.
- Cut a strip of lace about 8" (20 cm) long.
- Pull a thread in the heading of the lace until it fits the neckline of the bodice. If the chosen lace does not have a heading thread, sew a gathering thread by hand or machine and pull the thread until the lace fits the neckline.

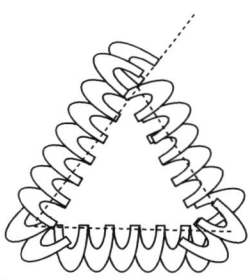

- Lay the right side of the lace on the wrong side of the fabric. The heading edge of the lace should be next to the raw edge of the fabric at the neckline.
- Adjust the machine setting to a short zigzag. The zigzag threads should be close enough together that they almost make a satin stitch. The zigzag should be the width of the lace heading.
- Zigzag the lace and fabric together.

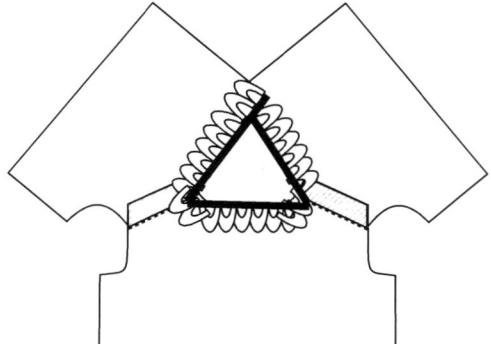

- Turn the lace to the right side of the fabric.

- Zigzag over the original zigzag seam.

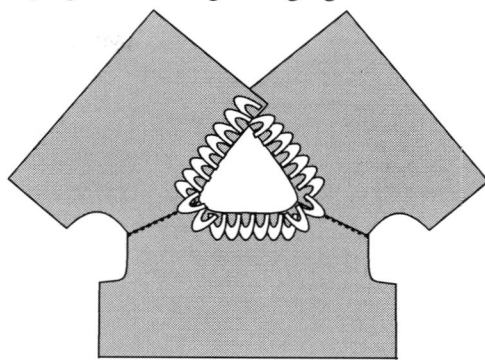

Facing a Neck Opening

Choose this method of finishing the neck for a simpler neckline.
- Sew both sets of bodice fronts to both sets of bodice backs at shoulders. Do not finish seams.
- Press seams open.
- Right sides together, pin the two bodices together at the neck.

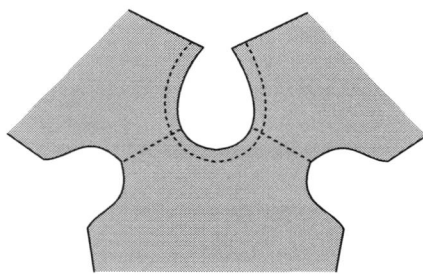

- Sew.
- Clip curves.
- Turn the bodice right side out and align the arm holes, sides, and bottom of bodice with the bodice facing.
- Press.
- Baste the bodice and facing together at arm holes and back opening.

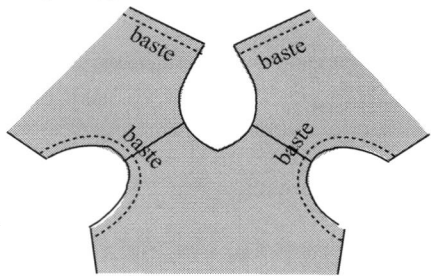

Making a Sleeve Casing and Adding Elastic

- To make each sleeve casing, press the finished casing edge of each sleeve ½" (12 mm) to the inside. Topstitch ¼" to ⅜" (6 to 9 mm) from the edge.
- Insert elastic into the casing and anchor one end of the elastic by sewing it down at one casing opening.
- Gather the casing fabric over the elastic to about 1⅞" (5 cm). Do not stretch the elastic.
- Check the fit around the wrist on the doll.

- Secure the second side of the elastic to the second casing opening by sewing through it and the casing several times. Cut off the excess elastic. (**Tips** p. 94)

Setting in the Sleeves

- Hand gather the top of each sleeve where indicated on the pattern.

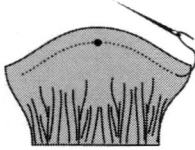

- Pull up the gathers to fit the arm hole of the bodice. Secure the gathering thread.
- Right sides together, pin and then hand baste each sleeve to the bodice. Match the dot at the top of the sleeve to the shoulder seams.
- Machine stitch each sleeve to the bodice.

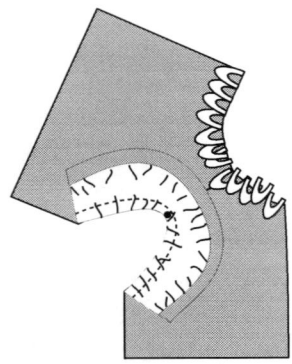

- Remove the basting and gathering stitches.
- Finish the seam with a zigzag stitch. A serger does not work well on such a small curve.

Sewing Bodice sides

- Fold right sides of bodice together at the shoulder seams.
- Sew across the bottom of each sleeve and down the bodice's side.

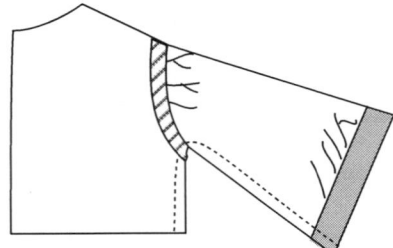

- Finish the seams.

Preparing the Skirt

If you have chosen to whip a hem in the dress, skip to *Gathering the Skirt*.

- Lay the right side of the lace chosen for the hem on the right side of the fabric. Do not gather the lace.
- The heading edge of the lace should be next to the raw edge of the skirt bottom.

- Adjust the machine setting to a short zigzag. The zigzag threads should be close enough together that they almost make a satin stitch. The zigzag should be the width of the lace heading.
- Zigzag the lace and fabric together.

- Pull the lace down below the fabric and press.
- The zigzagged seam will be on the inside of the skirt hem.

- Topstitch on the fabric very close to the lace using a straight stitch.

Gathering the Skirt

- Sew two rows of gathering stitches across the top of the skirt as indicated on the pattern.

- Pull up the gathering stitches to fit the bottom of the bodice

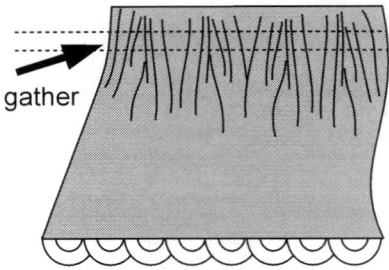

Attaching the Skirt to the Bodice

- Match the center fronts and pin the skirt to the bodice. You may baste them together if you like.

- Sew the skirt to the bodice.
- Remove the gathering stitches and optional basting stitches.
- Finish the seam.
- If you did not attach trim to the bottom of the skirt, whip in a ½" (12 mm) hem.

Sewing Trim to the Waist (optional)

- You may sew rickrack or other trim to the dress waist, if you like.
- Metallic rickrack sewn by hand with metallic pearl embroidery floss looks nice on the ballgown. Use plain rickrack on the classic dress.
- You could also tie a ribbon around the waist. The bow can go in either the front or back.

Closing the Back

- Finish the back seams.
- Press each back opening ½" (12 mm) to the inside.
- Apply hook and loop tape. (**Tips** p. **95**)

A-line Dress

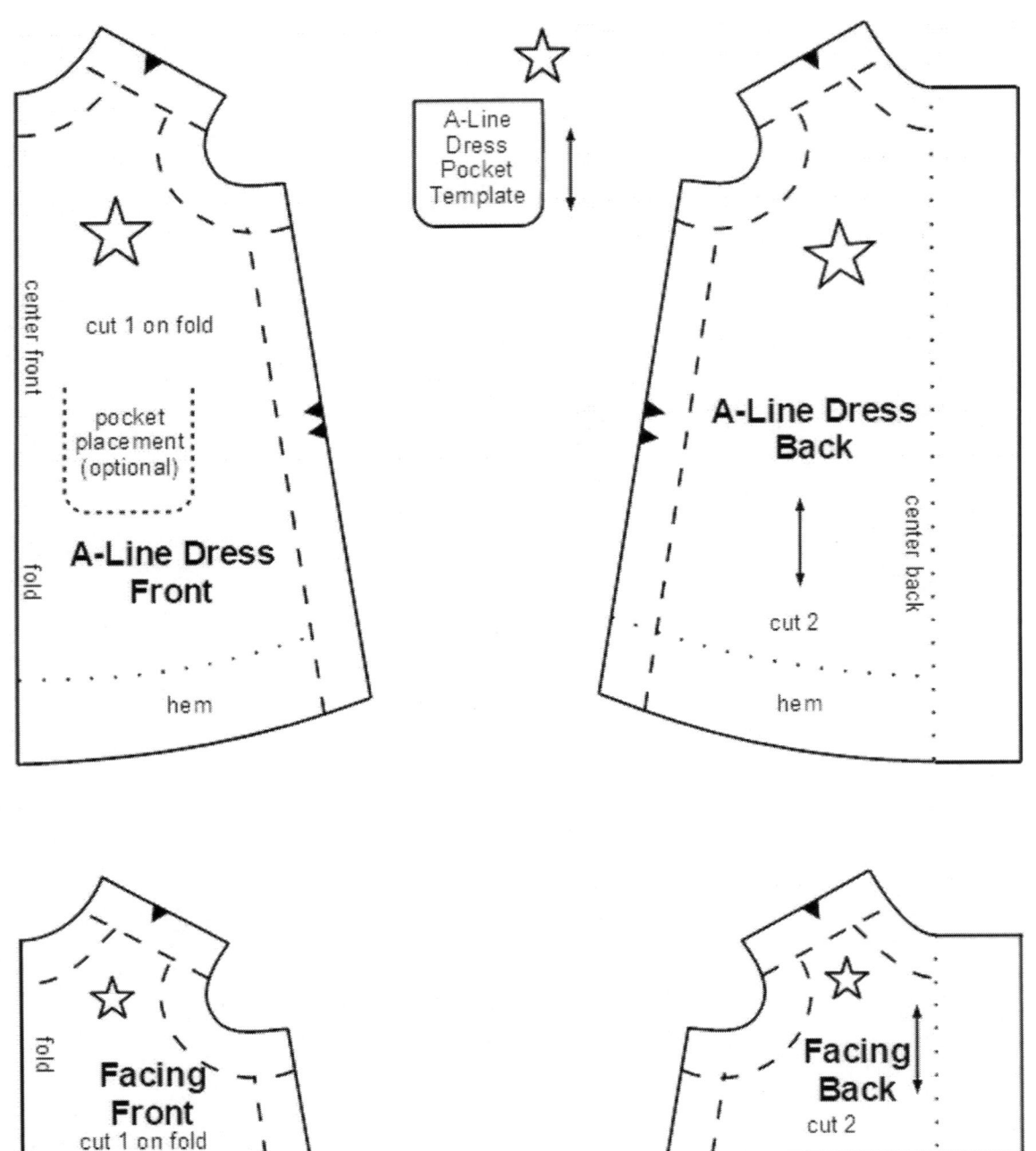

Sundress

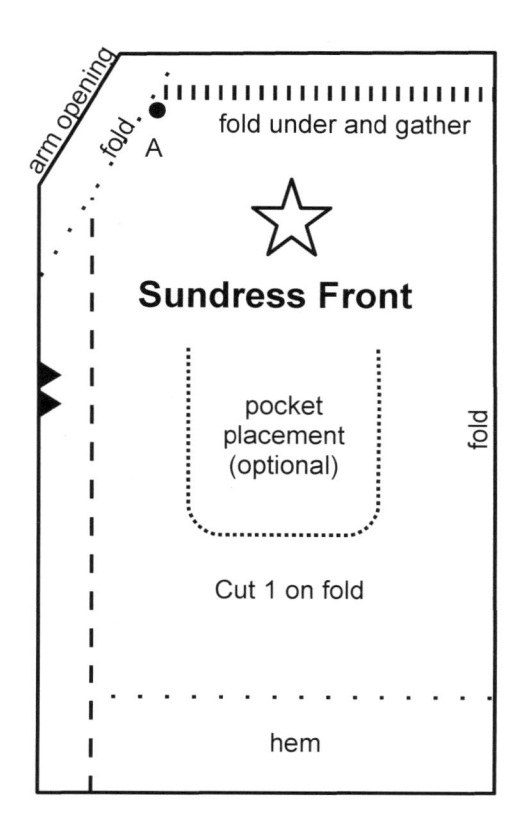

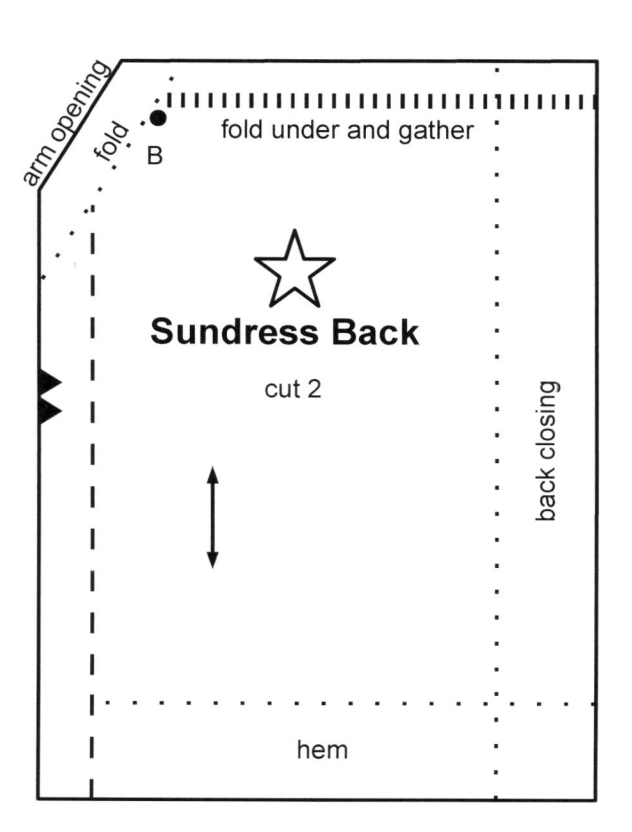

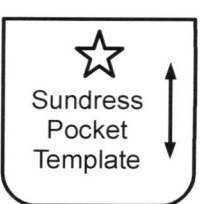

Classic Dress or Ballgown Bodice

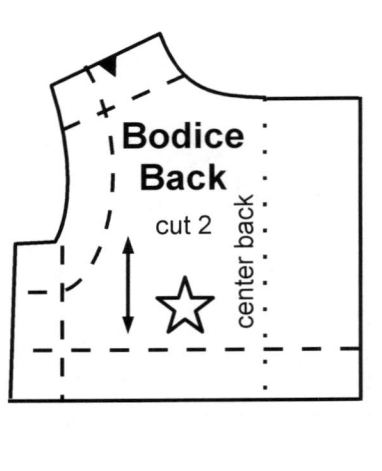

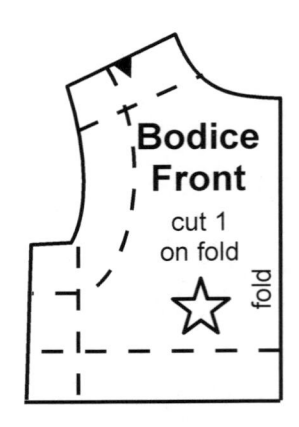

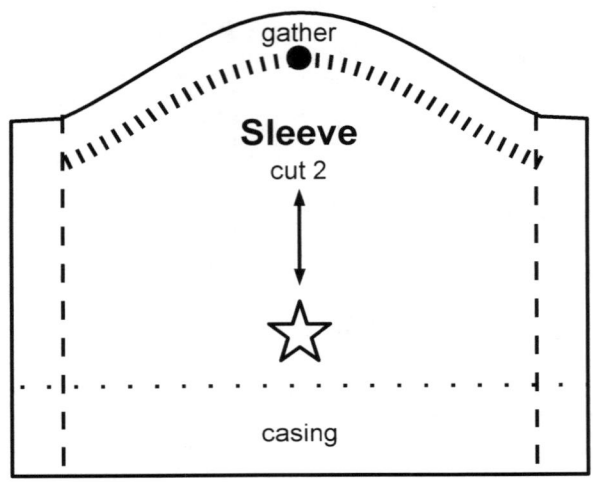

Classic Dress or Ballgown Skirt

center back

gather

☆ **Skirt**

Cut here for short skirt with lace

Cut here for short skirt with hem

Cut here for long skirt

fold

Short skirt with lace 2¼" x 6" (6 cm x 15 cm)
Short skirt with hem 2¾" x 6" (7 cm x 15 cm)
Long skirt 3¼" x 6" (8 cm x 15 cm)

Sewing for Mini Dolls
www.sherralynsdolls.com

Coats

The raincoat and the winter coat use the same pattern. Fabric choice and fasteners give a different look to each coat. The robe can be worn over the nightgown or nightshirt.

Raincoat

Winter Coat

Robe

Raincoat and Winter Coat

You will need: light weight cotton fabric for the raincoat. Yellow is a traditional raincoat fabric, but choose the color or print that you like. You will also need matching thread and hooks and eyes. For the winter coat you will need: cotton flannel, matching thread, and matching ⅜" (1 cm) buttons. After you have chosen your fabric, the directions for either coat are the same until you sew on the hooks and eyes or button holes and buttons.

Cutting and Marking

- Cut two fronts.
- Cut one back on the fold.
- Cut two collars.
- Mark the notches.
- Mark the A, B, C, and D dots.
- Do not clip the collar at this time.

Sewing Shoulder/Sleeve Seams

- With right sides together, match the A dots to the B dots and the front and back notches at the shoulders/sleeve top.

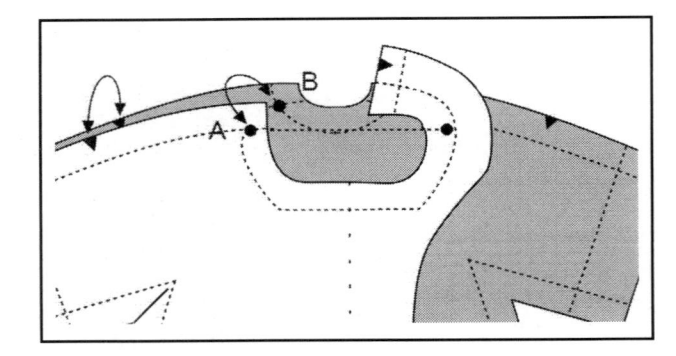

- Sew the shoulder seams. The point where the A and B dots join will now be called dot A/B.

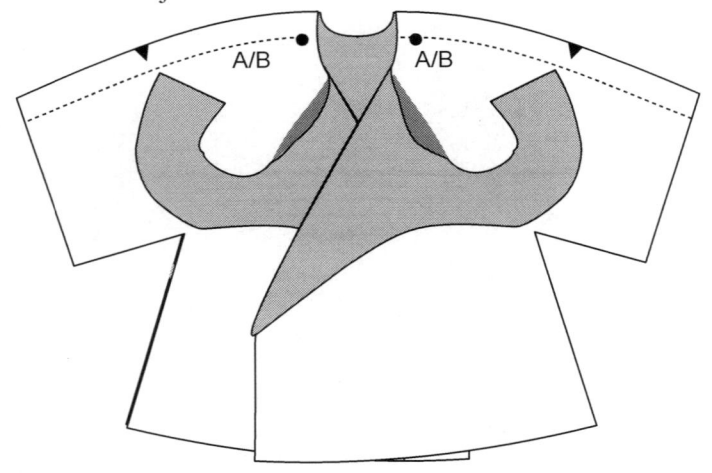

- Clip the seams.
- Press open. (I used a sleeve roll to press these seams.)

Construction the Collar

- With right sides together, sew the outer curve and the two short sides of the collar.

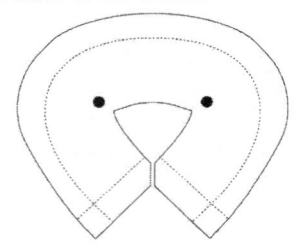

- Clip the corners and trim the seam.

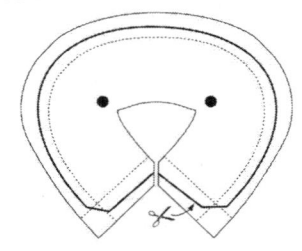

- Turn the collar right side out and press.
- Stay stitch the inner collar curve ¼" (6 mm) from the cut line.
- Clip collar where indicated on the pattern.

Applying the Collar and Facing

- With the collar on the outside of the coat, match the center back of the collar to the center back of the coat.
- Match the C dots to the A/B dots.
- Baste the collar to the coat.

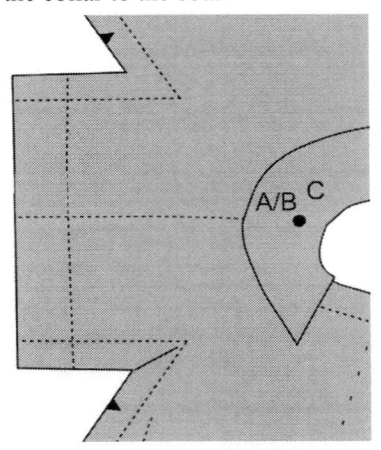

- With right sides together, match the facing notches and sew the facing seam.

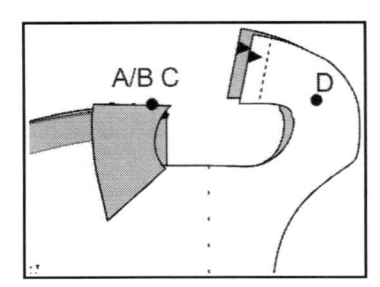

- Press the seam open.

42

- Match the facing seam to the center back of the coat and collar.
- Match the D dots to the C dot, A/B dot stack.
- Baste the facing to the collar and coat neck opening.

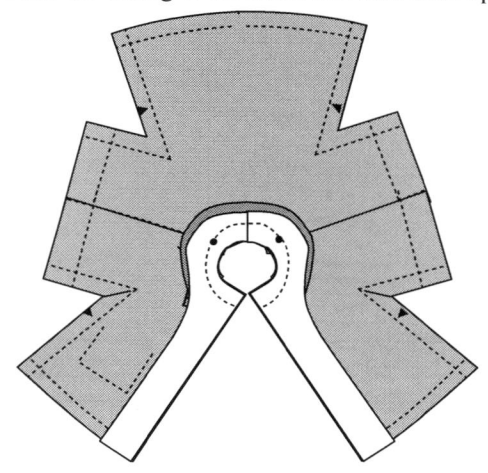

- Machine stitch the coat, collar, and facing together around the neck opening.
- Trim, turn, and press.
- If the facing will not lie flat, use a hand stitch at the seams, a small amount of fabric glue, or Elmer's® Xtreme® Glue Stick to hold it down.

Sewing the Sleeve Hems

- Finish the raw edges of the sleeve openings.
- Turn under ½" (12 mm).
- Press.
- Machine stitch the sleeve hem.

Adding Optional Pocket

- Use the instructions in *Square and Rectangular Pockets* (**Tips p. 95**).
- Add an optional pocket to the right side of the coat where indicated on the pattern.

Sewing the Side Seam

- With right sides together, match the side seam notches.
- Start sewing the sleeve/side seam at the sleeve edge.
- Use the needle down setting on your machine.
- Pivot the fabric on the needle to make a sharp angle with the stitching where the sleeve and side seams meet.

- Clip the sleeve/side seam where indicated on the pattern.

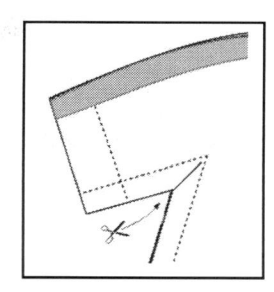

- Turn the coat right side out and press.

Hemming the Raincoat or Coat

- Finish the bottom edge of the raincoat or coat.
- Run a gathering stitch around the finished bottom edge of the coat.
- Press a ¼" (6 mm) hem in the coat.
- Pull the gathering stitch as you press, so that the hem lies flat inside the coat.
- Machine stitch the hem.

Adding Hooks and Eyes to the Raincoat

- Use the *Hook Placement Guide* to position and sew hooks to the right front side of the raincoat.
- Position a round eye on the left front side of the raincoat to catch each hook.
- Sew each rounded eye to the left side of the raincoat.

Adding Button Holes and Buttons to the Winter Coat

- Mark button placement from coat front pattern on the right front side of the winter coat.
- Sew the button holes using your machine's instructions.
- Using the button holes that you have made, mark the correct placement of the buttons on the left front of the coat.
- Sew buttons to left front of the coat.

Robe

You will need: cotton flannel, knit ribbing, and matching thread. If you can't find ribbing, try using a stretchy knit fabric.

Cutting and Marking

- Cut two fronts.
- Cut one back on the fold.
- Cut out tie belt.
- Cut out front and sleeve ribbing.
- Mark the notches.

Sewing Shoulder/Sleeve Seams

- With right sides together, match the front and back notches at the shoulders/sleeve top.

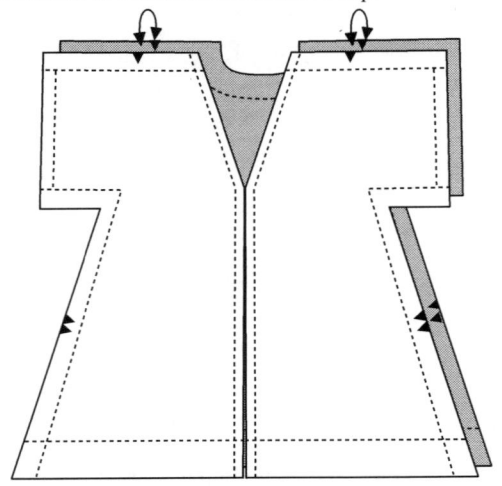

- Sew the shoulder seams.
- Press open

Sewing the Ribbing

- Fold each ribbing piece in half lengthwise and press.
- On the right side of the fabric, lay the front ribbing piece on the robe. Match the raw edges.
- Sew the ribbing all the way around the center front opening and neck, using an ⅛" (3 mm) seam.

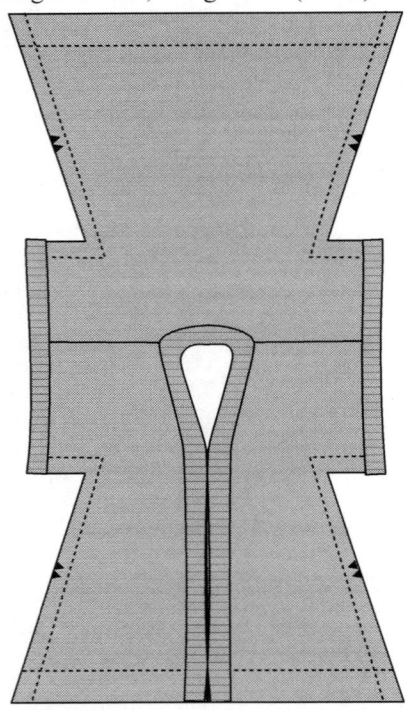

- Sew one small ribbing piece to each sleeve edge.
- Press the robe and ribbing so that the seam is inside the robe and the ribbing is on the outside of the robe..
- Topstitch at the very edge of the robe fabric next to the ribbing.

Sewing the Side Seam

- With right sides together, match the side seam notches.
- Start sewing the sleeve/side seam at the sleeve edge.
- Use the needle down setting on your machine.
- Pivot the fabric on the needle to make a sharp angle with the stitching where the sleeve and side seams meet.
- Clip the sleeve/side seam where indicated on the pattern.

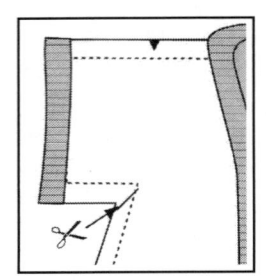

- Turn the robe right side out and press.

Hemming the Robe

- Press a ½" (12 mm) hem in the robe.
- Machine stitch the hem.

Sewing the Tie Belt

- Fold the belt fabric in half lengthwise, right sides together.
- Press.
- Sew. Leave the turning opening indicated on the pattern.
- Clip corners and turn right side out.
- Slip-stitch or machine stitch the turning opening closed.

Raincoat and Winter Coat

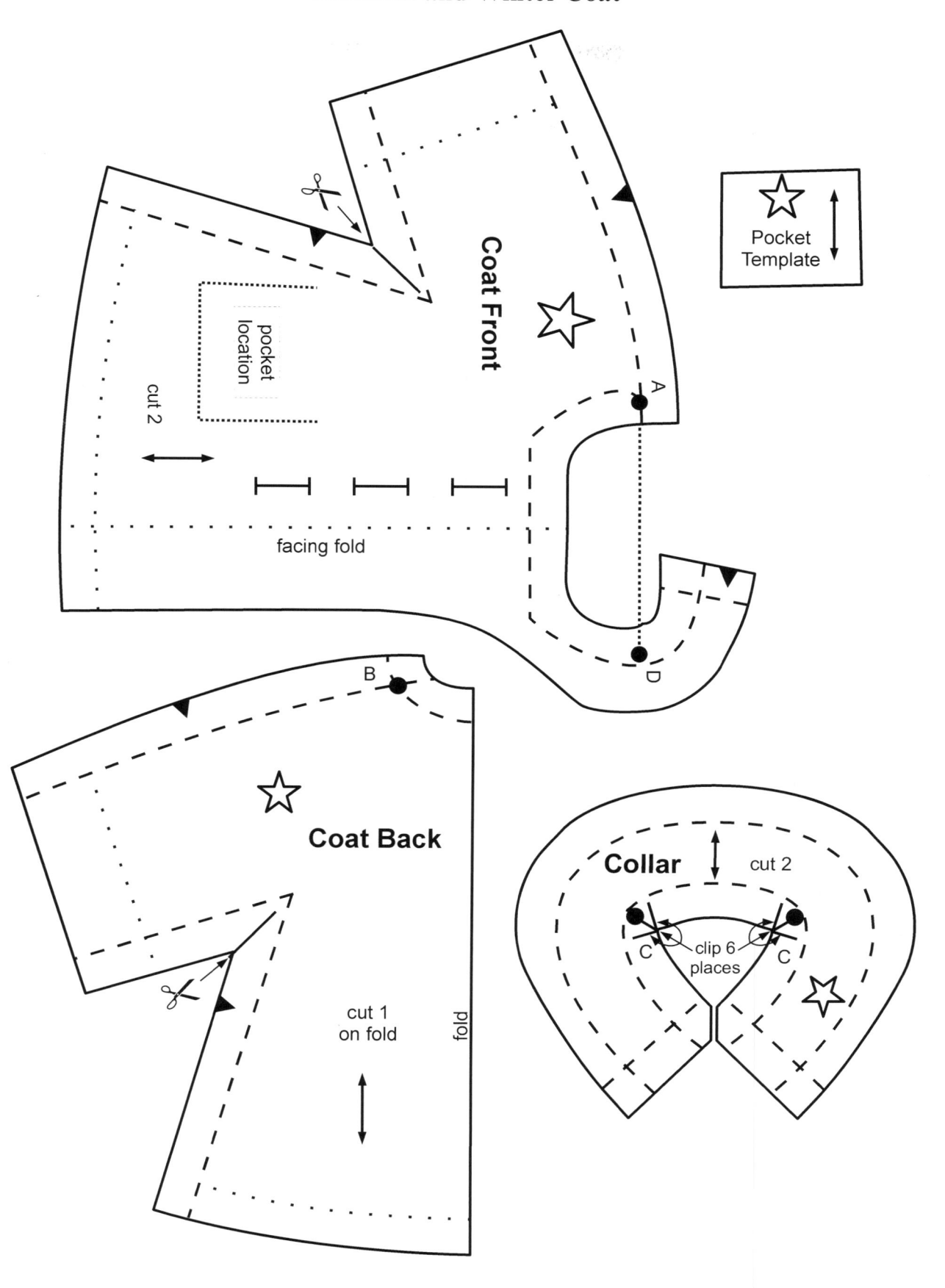

Coat Front — cut 2

pocket location

facing fold

A

D

Pocket Template

Coat Back — cut 1 on fold

B

fold

Collar — cut 2

clip 6 places

C   C

45

Raincoat Hook Placement and Robe Ribbing and Belt

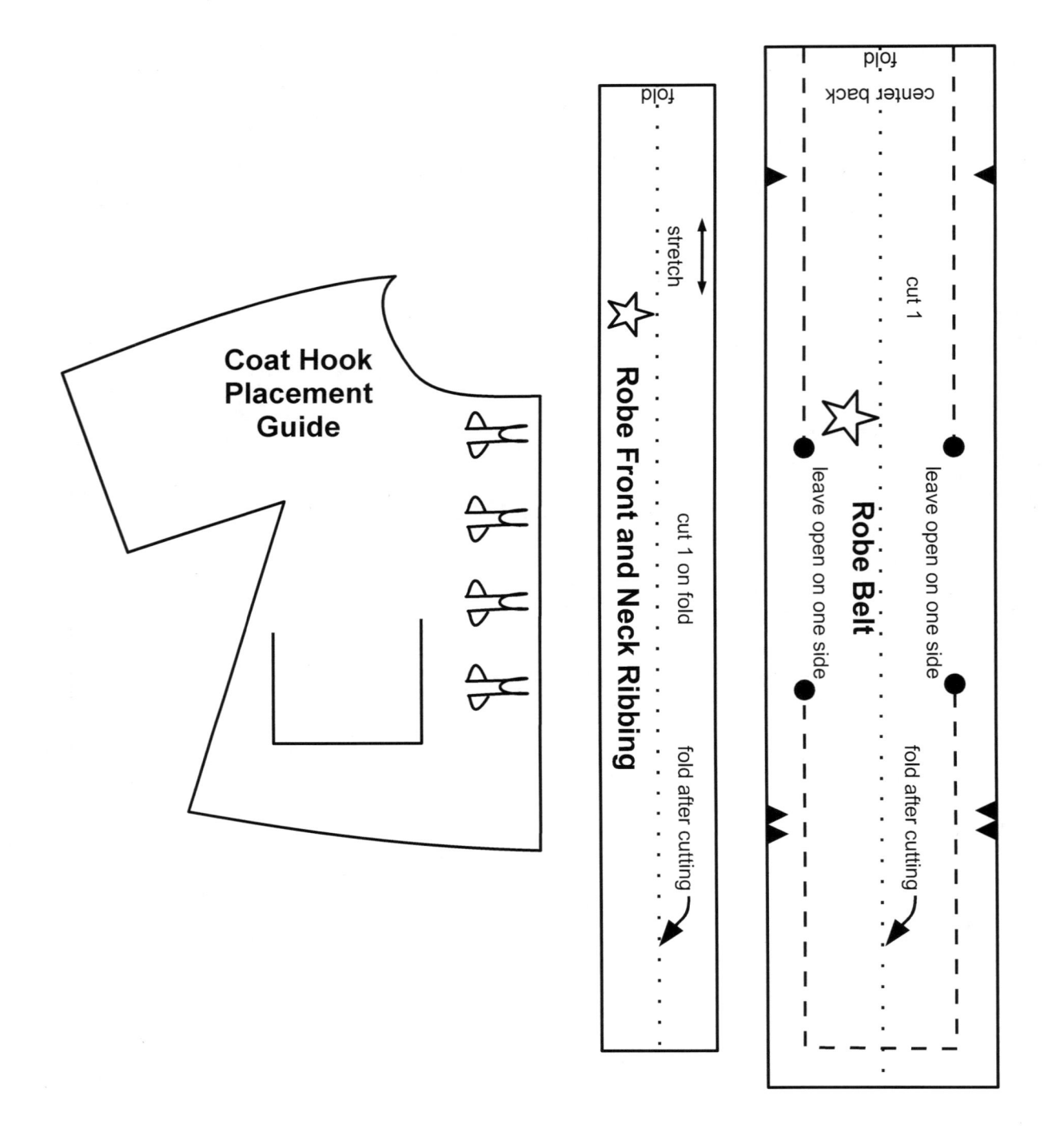

46

Robe

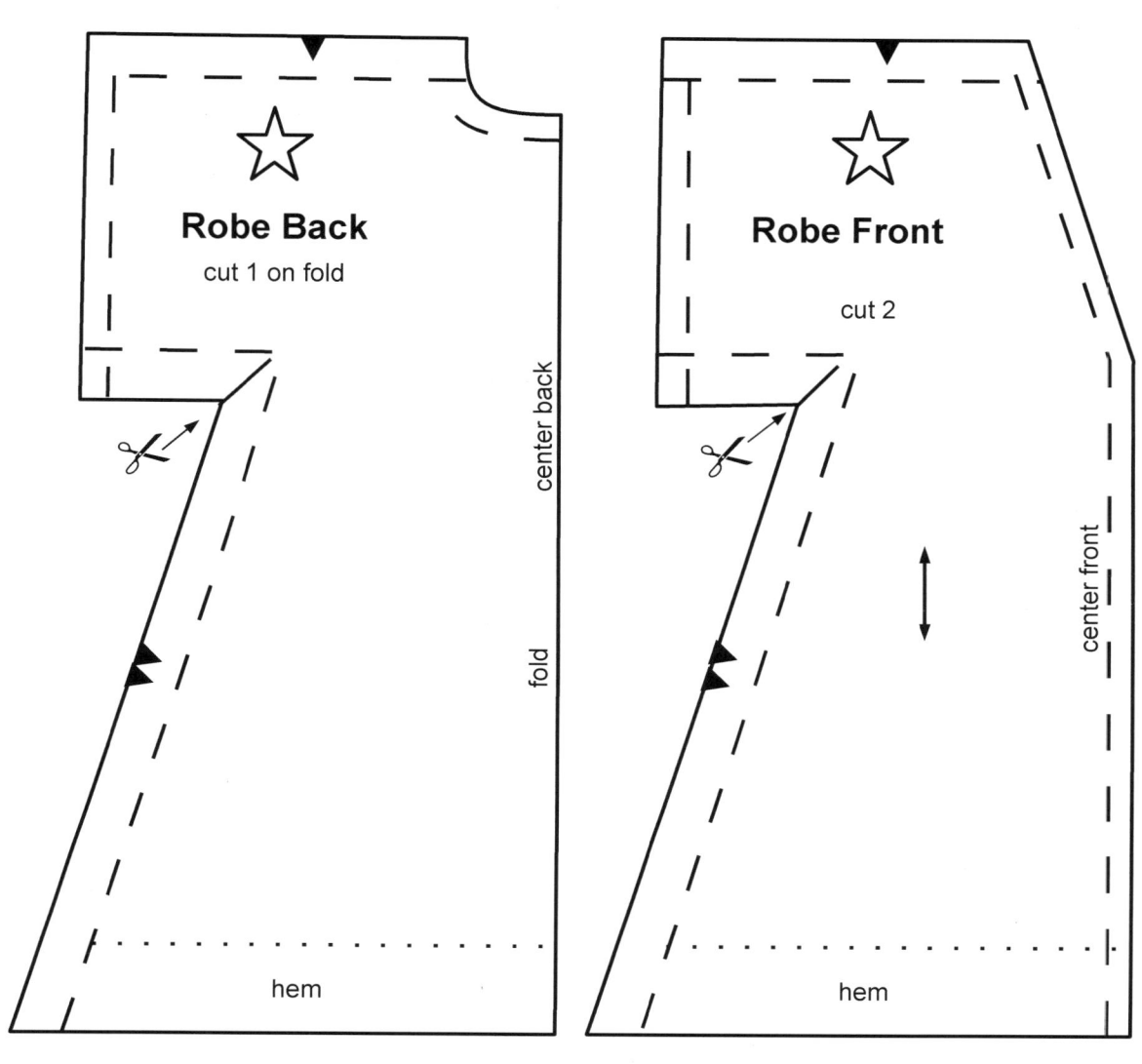

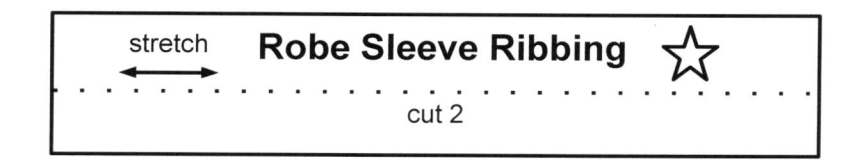

Robe Back — cut 1 on fold

Robe Front — cut 2

Robe Sleeve Ribbing — cut 2

Sewing for Mini Dolls
www.sherralynsdolls.com

Extras

The extras in this book are here to add extra fun to doll dressing, doll collecting, and doll play. The collection of footwear includes shoes, bunny and mouse slippers, sneakers, and boots. Hats include a nightcap, a rain or sun hat, and a princess crown. Totes include a purse and a backpack. This chapter it ends with instructions for a working umbrella and an all cloth doll bed with its bedding.

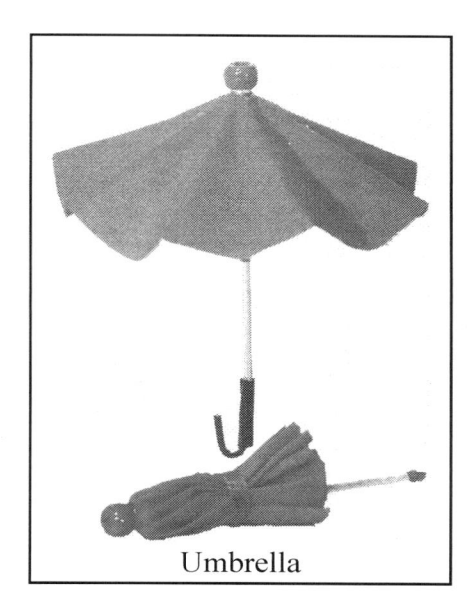

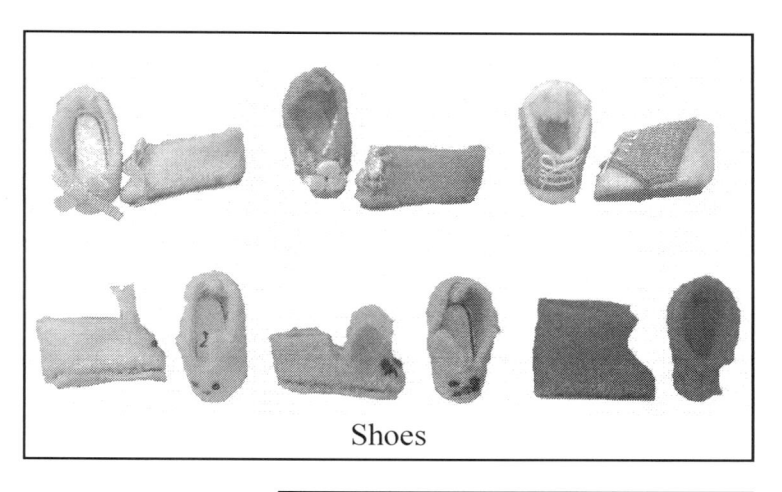

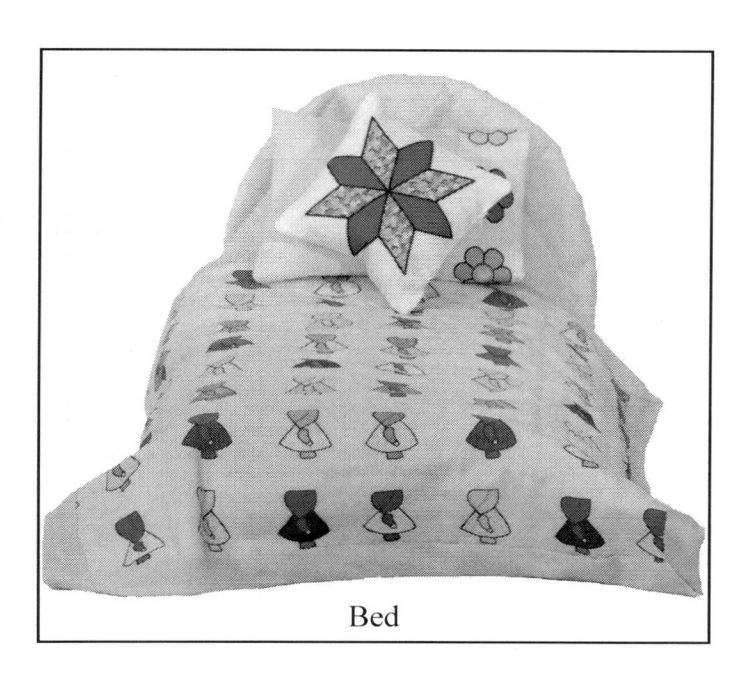

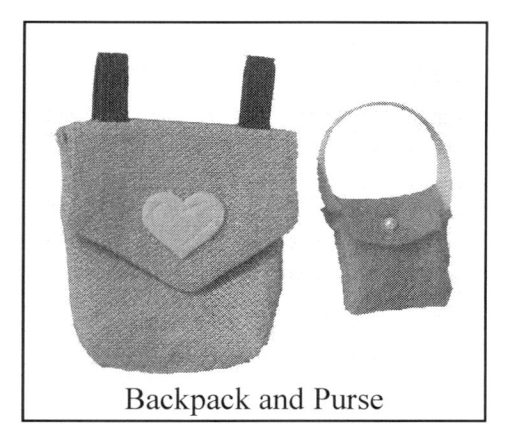

Umbrella

Shoes

Rain or Sun Hat, Stocking Nightcap, and Princess Crown

Bed

Backpack and Purse

Shoes

You will need:
- Felt in the color of your choice for slippers, shoes, sneakers, and boots
- Woven fabric in the color of your choice for sneaker overlays
- Sewable fusible inner facing for sneaker overlay
- Seam sealant
- Felt (I like stiff felt.) or light cardboard (I use the squares that come with fat quarters.) for soles
- Index card or light cardboard for insole
- Elmer's® Xtreme® Glue Stick or Tacky Glue®
- Optional buttons, bows, or small appliques for shoes
- Pearl cotton for sneaker laces
- Black embroidery floss for the bunny and mouse slipper eyes and the mouse's whiskers
- Pink embroidery floss for bunny and mouse slipper noses
- Two pink or white ¼" (6 mm) pompoms for bunny slipper tails (optional)

Dress Shoe

Cutting
- Cut out two shoes from felt.

Sewing Shoes
- Stay-stitch the bottom of the shoe ¼" (6 mm) from the raw edge. The fabric below the stay-stitch line will be turned under and glued to the sole and insole.

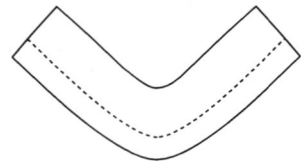

- Topstitch around the top of the shoe (optional)

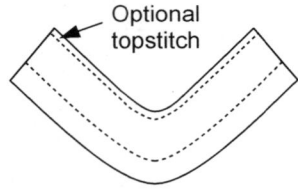

  Optional topstitch

- Right sides together, bring the two short sides of the shoe together. Sew an ⅛" (3 mm) seam to make the shoe heel.
- Turn the shoe right side out.

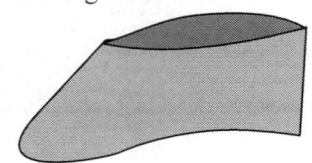

- Go to the section titled **Gluing the Sole and Insole**.

Slippers

If you are making slippers from Spoonflower fabric, start on p. 84.

Cutting
- Cut two slippers from felt. Make sure that you cut around the entire ear cut line for both the bunny and the mouse. The mouse ears will not stand out if they are not cut correctly. Follow directions on the pattern.

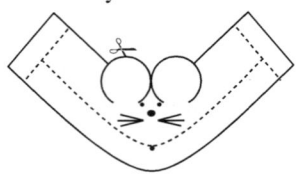

Making Facial Features
- Mark the eyes and nose on the right side of the felt with air soluble pen.
- Make a French knot for each eye using two strands of floss.
- Make a French knot for the mouse's nose using two strands of pink floss.
- Use three or five stitches with two strands of pink floss to make a triangular nose for the bunny.
- Take a long stitch with black floss for each of the mouse's whiskers.

Sewing Slipper
- Stay-stitch the bottom of each slipper ¼" (6 mm) from the raw edge. The fabric below the stay-stitch line will be turned under and glued to the sole and insole.

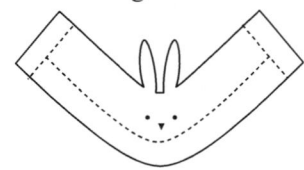

- Right sides together, bring the two short sides of the slipper together. Sew an ⅛" (3 mm) seam to make the slipper heel.
- Turn the slipper right side out.

- Go to the section titled **Gluing the Sole and Insole**.

Sneakers

If you are making sneakers from Spoonflower fabric, start on p. 85.

Cutting

- Cut out two sneakers from white or other colored felt.
- Cut two overlays from fusible inner facing.
- Cut a piece of fabric in the color of your choice large enough for both overlays.

Preparing the Overlay

- Bond the two cut out fusible inner facing overlays to the chosen overlay fabric.
- Cut out.
- Mark the eyelet holes with air soluble pen.

Sewing the Sneaker

- Line up the Overlay with the top of the sneaker. Glue the sneaker overlay to the right side of the sneaker.

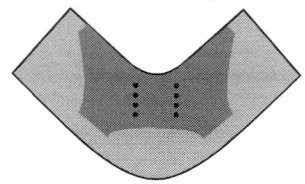

- Stay-stitch the bottom of the sneaker ¼" (6 mm) from the raw edge. The fabric below the stay-stitch line will be turned under and glued to the sole and insole.
- Use a narrow, close zigzag stitch to stitch around the outside of the overlay.

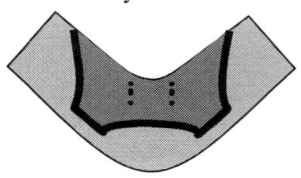

Adding Laces

- Use a large needle to push through each of the eyelet holes marked on the sneaker.
- Thread the needle with pearl cotton and pull the cotton through the eyelets like a shoe lace.

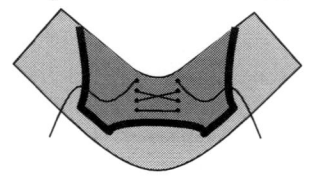

- Tie the cotton lace in a bow and trim the excess.
- Use white glue on the center of the bow to prevent it from coming untied.
- Right sides together, bring the two short sides of the sneaker together. Sew an ⅛" (3 mm) seam to make the sneaker heel.
- Turn the shoe right side out.

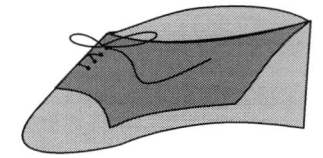

- Go to the section titled **Gluing the Sole and Insole.**

Boot

Cutting and Marking

- Cut out two boots
- Mark the dots labeled A and B.
- The B dot marks the center back and the middle of the heel. It is helpful when attaching the insole and sole.

Sewing the Boot

- Stay-stitch the bottom of the boot ¼" (6 mm) from the raw edge. The fabric below the stay-stitch line will be turned under and glued to the sole and insole.
- Fold the boot right sides together.
- Start the A dot and sew the toe seam.

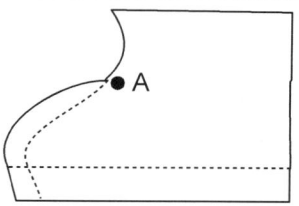

- Turn the boot right side out.
- Go to the section titled **Gluing the Sole and Insole.**

Gluing the Sole and Insole

In this part of the instructions the word "vamp" refers to the top part of the shoe, slipper, sneaker, or boot.

- Cut two insoles from an index card or light cardboard.
- Cut two soles from felt or light cardboard.
- Clip the bottom of the vamp in the four places shown on the pattern. Stop each clip at the stay-stitching. For Spoonflower sneaker stop the clip where the lining begins.
- Hand stitch and gather the heel and toe fabric at the bottom of the vamp until it curls around to the lining or the slipper's stay-stitching. The stitching should be very close to the cut edge.

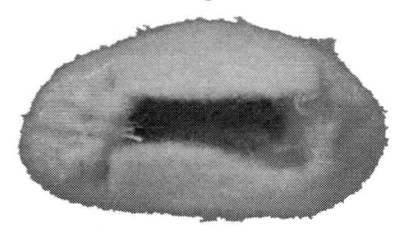

- Insert insole into the vamp.

- Glue the vamp bottom to the insole. Use the doll's foot, the eraser side of a pencil, or other stick to press the vamp and insole together.
- Glue the sole to the outside of the vamp against the insole, hiding the insole and the vamp bottom.

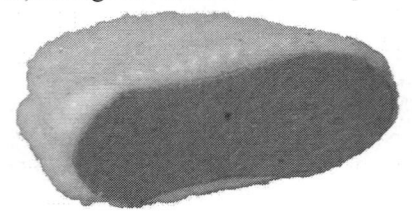

Rain Hat or Sun Hat

Yellow is a traditional rain hat fabric, but choose the color or print that you like. You might also want to make a sun hat. I made a hat from khaki colored fabric for a doll to wear outside in the sun when studying things such as insects or rocks.

You will need: light weight, woven cotton fabric and matching thread.

Cutting and Marking

- Cut 4 crown sections.
- Cut two brims.
- Mark the notches on each side of the brim center back seam.

Sewing the Crown

- The four crown sections are called A, B, C, and D here. 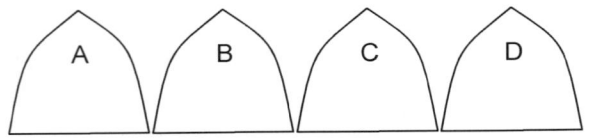
- With right sides together, match one side of each pair of crown sections.
- Sew the A and B crown sections together on one side to make AB. Repeat for C and D to make CD.
- Open up crown section pairs AB and CD. With right sides together, match the two pair of crown sections AB and CD. 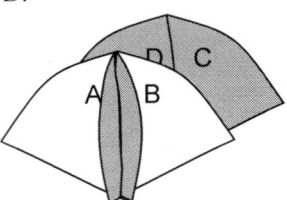
- Sew crown section B to crown section C. 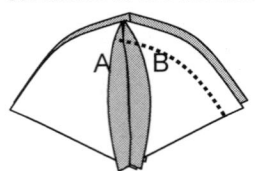
- Do not sew the fourth side of the hat crown together, yet.

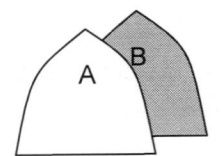

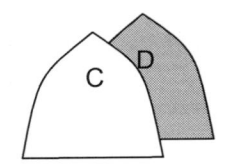

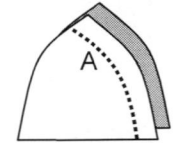

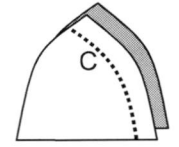

Sewing the Brim

- With right sides together, sew the two brim pieces together along the outer curve. 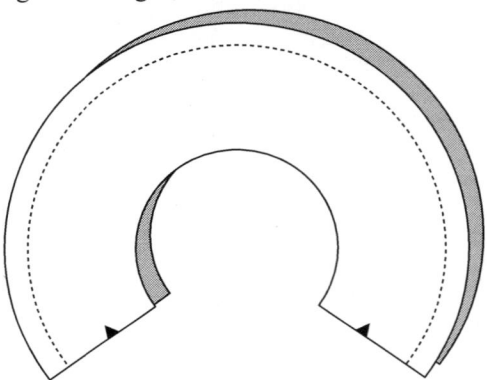
- Trim the outer curve, turn, and press.
- You may topstitch parallel to the outer brim, if you like. The first topstitching row is suggested on the pattern as ¼" (6 mm) from the outer edge. You can have only one row of topstitching, or you can add several more rows of stitching, or you can leave out the topstitching.
- Stay-stitch the inner curve of the brim.
- Clip the curve about every ¼" (6 mm).

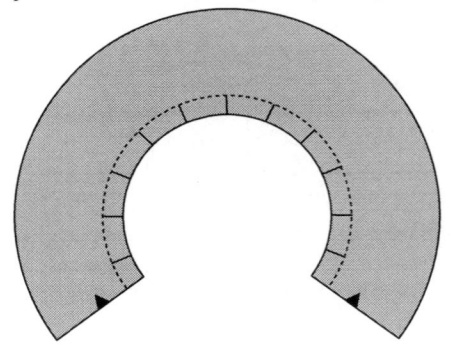

Sewing the Crown to the Brim

- Starting at the center back, with right sides together, pin, and then baste the crown to the brim.
- Machine stitch the crown to the brim. 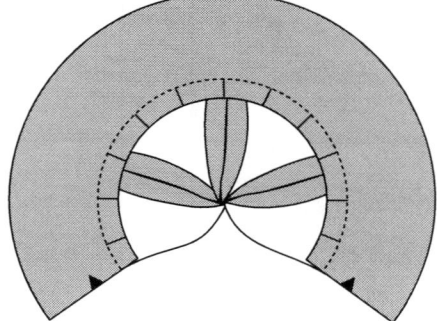
- With right sides together, starting at the top of the crown, baste the center back seam closed. 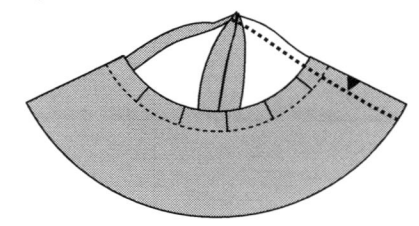
- Machine stitch the center back seam.
- Turn the hat right side out.

Insect Net

If you made a sun hat and want an insect net to go with it, free instructions for the net can be found at www.sherralynsdolls.com. Select Florabunda's page from the buttons at the top of the main page. On Florabunda's page select easy craft projects from that page's directory.

Stocking Nightcap

You will need: a fairly thin lady's sock; a 13 mm pompom; and matching thread for hand sewing.

Measuring and Cutting

- Measure down from the top of the sock about 6" (15 cm). 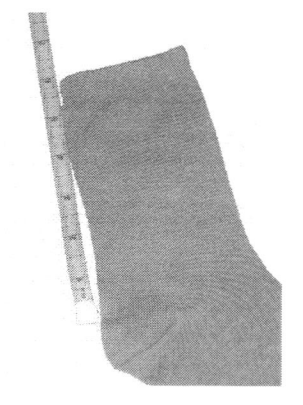
- Cut across the sock to make two pieces: a tube and a piece containing the heel and toe. 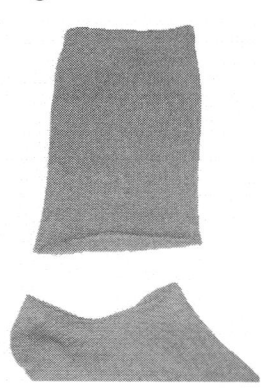
- Use the heel and toe of the sock for another project. The nightcap will be made from the tube.

Hand Sewing the Nightcap

- Turn the tube wrong side out.
- Hand gather all the way around the cut edge of the tube.
- Pull the gathers until the raw edge of the tube is completely closed to make a cap. I like to go over the gathering several times and secure the thread each time. I think that effort gives the hand sewing more strength. 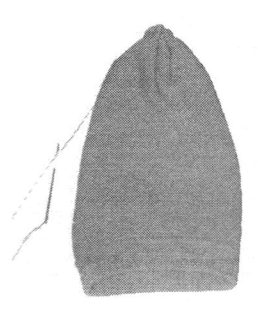
- Turn the cap right side out.
- Sew or glue a pompom over the gathered end.

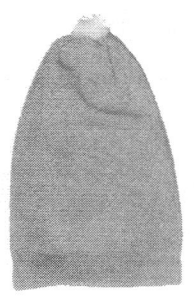

Princess Crown

This Crown is an easy and enjoyable project. To make it, you will need to sew a few hand stitches and glue on the royal jewels.

- Measure around the doll's head where she will wear the crown.

- Cut a length of trim ¼" (6 mm) longer than the measurement.

- Cut an optional higher front for the crown. The length should be ¼" (6 mm) longer than the finished length of the front piece.
- Add seam sealant to the ends.

- If you have cut a higher front piece, turn under the seam allowances and sew it to the middle of the crown.

- Glue on the jewels.

- Turn under a ⅛" (3 mm) seam allowance, and sew the ends together to make a circle.

Purse

You will need: a scrap of felt, ⅛" (3 mm) wide ribbon, a small bead, and matching thread. You will need a seam ripper and a disappearing ink pen.

Cutting and Sewing

- Cut out the purse from felt.
- Fold the purse where indicated on the pattern.

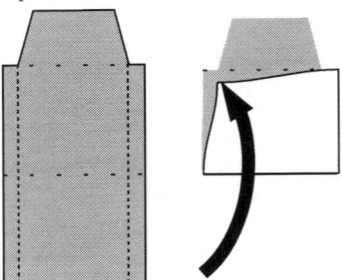

- Sew the two purse side seams.

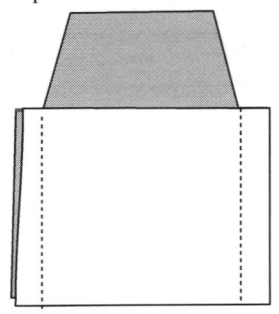

Sewing the purse strap

- Cut a piece or ribbon 3" (8 cm) long for a strap.

- Sew one side of the strap at the top of each side seam by hand.

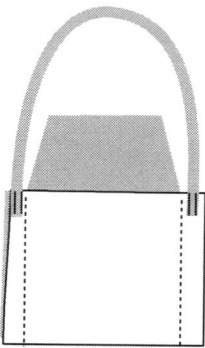

- Turn the purse right side out.

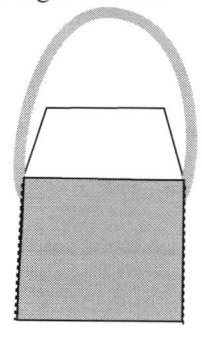

Adding the Fastener

- Punch a small hole with a seam ripper on the purse flap, indicated by a black dot on the pattern.
- Fold the flap over the purse.
- Use a disappearing marker to mark through the small hole onto the purse.
- Sew on the bead where you have made the mark.

Backpack

You will need: a small piece of woven cotton, ¼" (6 mm) wide elastic (I used black elastic), a small piece of hook and loop tape, an optional small applique, and matching thread.

Cutting and Marking

- Cut one backpack.
- Cut two flaps.
- Cut two 3" (7.6 cm) strips of elastic.
- Mark the double notches on the back and flaps.
- Mark the placement of elastic and hook and loop tape.

Sewing the Flap

- Sew around the flap leaving the straight side marked with double notches open.

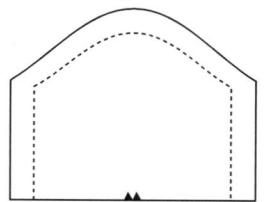

- Trim the seam: turn the flap: and press.

Attaching the Flap, Elastic, and Hook and Loop Tape

- Place seam sealant on the four cut ends of the elastic.
- Allow to dry.
- On the right side of the fabric, place one end of each elastic piece on the double notches side of the backpack, where indicated on the pattern.

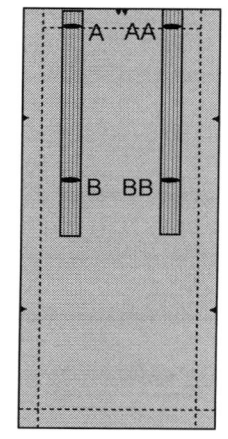

- Lay the flap on the right side of the fabric on top of the elastic. Match the raw edges and the double notches.
- Sew the flap and the top of the elastic pieces to the backpack.

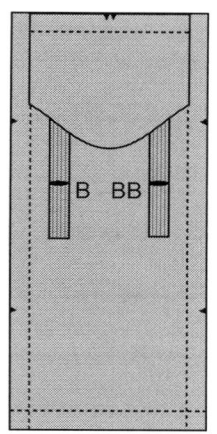

55

- Sew the backpack piece of hook and loop tape where indicated on the pattern.
- Sew the bottom of the elastic pieces to the backpack where indicated on the pattern.

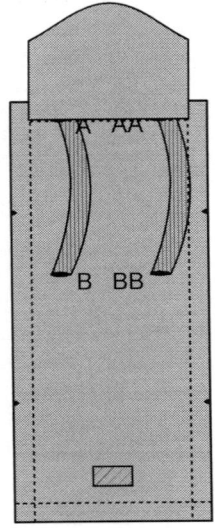

- Turn under ¼" of fabric on the short side of the backpack opposite of the flap and hem where indicated on the pattern.

Finishing the Backpack

- Right sides together, fold the backpack where indicated on the pattern. Sew the side seams.

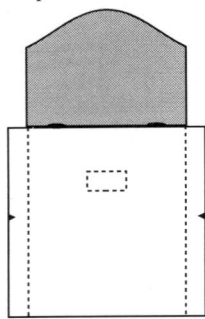

- Before turning the backpack right side out, finger press the sides seams open and sew across each bottom corners to give the backpack a flat bottom. (optional)
- Turn right side out.
- Sew hook and loop tape to flap where indicated on the pattern.
- Sew or glue an applique on the flap if you like.

Umbrella

This umbrella is fun to make, but it is not a safe toy for very young children. Also, it is a delicate object, and will not last through vigorous play even from children in appropriate age groups. It should be used for display or very gentle play.

You will need: a 4" (10 cm) cocktail umbrella; a small piece of woven cotton, seam sealant, matching thread, and fabric glue or Elmer's Xtreme Glue Stick to attach ribs to the cover. Optional materials include: a ⅜" (9 mm) pony bead and glue to attach it for a top cap; a paper clip, wire cutters, and narrow colored tape for a handle ; and craft paint or clear finger nail polish for ribs.

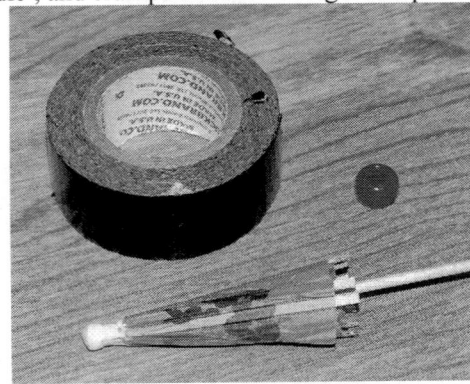

Colored tape, a cocktail umbrella, and a pony bead

Preparing the Umbrella

- Remove the paper umbrella cover from its ribs. I like to cut the paper between each rib and remove the paper a section at a time.
- If you would like to cap the top of your umbrella with a pony bead, check for fit. You may need to scrape some of the paint and paper off the current cap to get the fit that you need. When you are sure of the fit, remove the bead. You will replace it after you have secured the cover to the ribs.
- To strengthen the rib/stretcher frame of the umbrella, paint it with gray or silver craft paint or clear fingernail polish (optional).

Cutting and Pressing the Umbrella Cover

- Cut one umbrella cover.
- Carefully add seam sealant to the outside edge and let dry.
- The cover needs to be folded and pressed until it is divided into eight equal sections. All of the creases need to be in the same direction. To press the cover correctly, you will need to open and refold the circle in half each time you press it.
  - Fold the circle cover in half, matching the AA line on the pattern.
  - Press a crease in the fold.

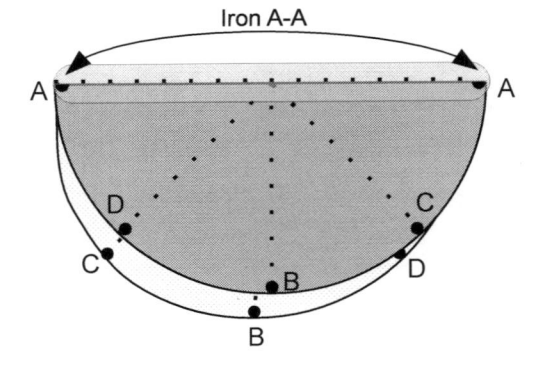

- Open the cover and fold in half again. This time fold on the BB line. Make sure that the AA line is creased outward.

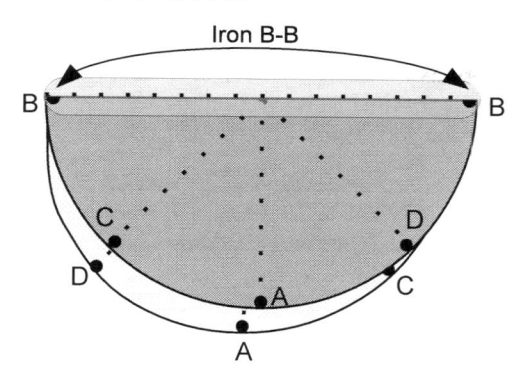

Iron B-B

- Press the new crease in the cover, dividing the cover into quarters. Use the tip of your iron to make sure that you only disturb the AA crease where the AA and and BB line cross at the center of the circle.
- Open the cover and fold in half again. This time fold on the CC line. Make sure that the AA line and the BB line are creased outward.

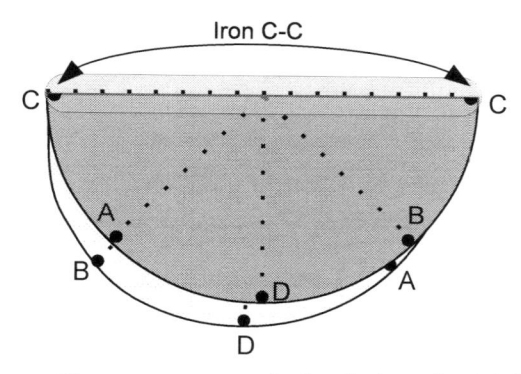

Iron C-C

- Press a new crease in the circle at the CC line. Use the tip of your iron to make sure that you only disturb the other creases at the center of the circle at the intersection of the creases.
- Finish your pressing by pressing an outward crease on the DD line.

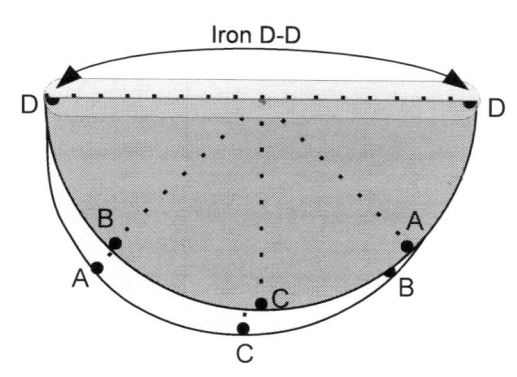

Iron D-D

Attaching the Cover to the Ribs

- Cut a small hole in the center of the cover, as indicated on the pattern. All of the folds on the right side of the umbrella cover should be creased outward.

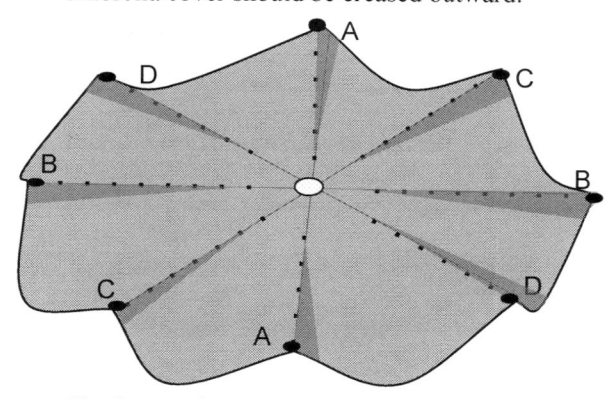

- Check to make sure that the cap at the top of the umbrella frame will fit through the small center hole that you have just cut.
- Add seam sealant around the center cut and allow to dry.
- Choose a pair of ribs that together mark the diameter of the circle. There should be three ribs on either side of this rib pair.

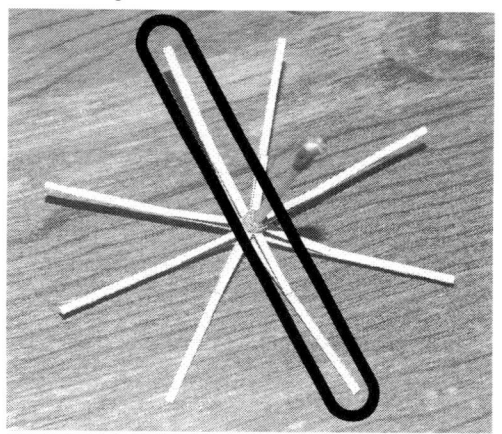

- Place the cover on the ribs making sure that the center hole is below the cap. All of the creases should be facing out so that a rib can be glued to the underside of each crease.
- Glue or sew the two ribs to the inside crease of line AA.
- Find the crease that follows the line BB.

- Attach the appropriate ribs to the inside crease of line BB.

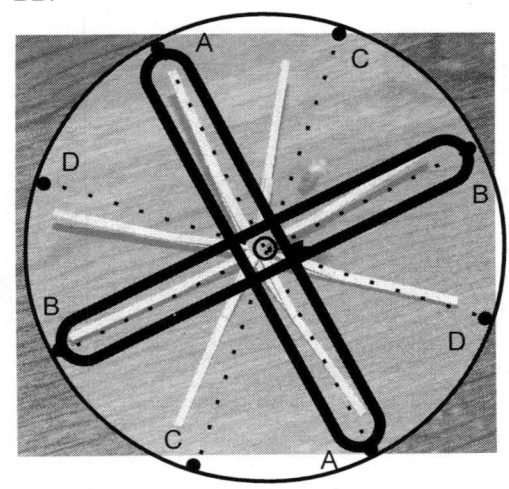

- There should be one loose rib between each attached rib.
- Attach the remaining ribs to the appropriate inside crease. Align these ribs to match the creases you pressed in.

Adding a Cap and Handle (Optional)

- If you are using a pony bead for the top cap, glue it over the original cap.
- To make a handle, you can use wire cutters to snip a J shape from a paper clip.
    - Use a plastic coated clip or paint the area of the clip that you will use as a handle.
    - Use narrow colored tape to attach the handle to the umbrella.
- For a simpler handle, wrap narrow colored tape at the bottom of the umbrella shaft until it reaches the desired thickness.

Doll Bed

Dolls up to 9" (23 cm) tall can use this bed.

You will need:
- Quilted fabric for bed and headboard
- 1" (2.5 cm) thick foam for bed
- Plastic canvas for bed
- Quilt batting for headboard and mattress
- Fabric for mattress and pillow
- Polyester stuffing for pillow
- Fabric for the top and back of cover
- Double fold bias tape for optional quilted cover.
- Two coordinating fabrics for two tone pillowcase
- Craft tool for cutting plastic canvas (Wire cutters work well for this job.)
- A rotary cutter and cutting mat for cutting straight lines (optional). A rotary cutter and cutting mat are very good tools for accurately cutting straight fabric pieces. They are useful for cutting out the pieces of this doll bed. Use them if you have them.

- If you do not have a rotary cutter, you will need a ruler, marking pencil or chalk, and scissors to cut all the pieces of the bed to the dimensions given.

The Bed

All construction of the bed and bed clothing will use a ¼" (6 mm) seam allowance.

Cutting and Marking

- Cut out two bed tops and bottoms from quilted fabric.
    - 9⅝" by 6" (24 cm by 15 cm)
- Cut out two sides from quilted fabric.
    - 9⅝" by 1¾" (24 cm by 4 cm)
- Cut out one head-of-the-bed and one bed foot from quilted fabric.
    - 6" by 1¾" (15 cm by 4 cm)

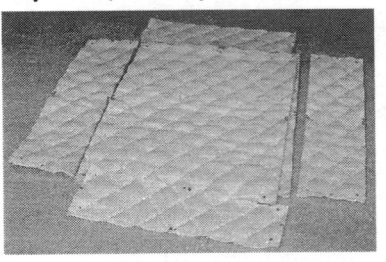

- Cut one bed insert from foam and two bed inserts from plastic canvas.
    - 8½" by 5" (26.5 cm by 13 cm)
- Mark the dots on the bed sides and head and foot pieces as indicated on the figure below. The dots should be at each point where two ¼" (6 mm) seam allowances meet.

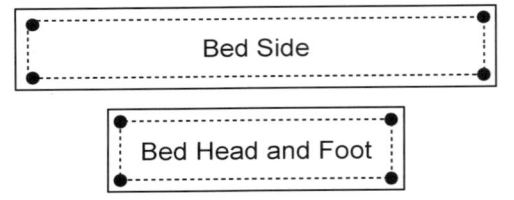

Sewing the Bed Sides

- Sew one head/foot piece to the bed side pieces, beginning and ending on the dots. Don't sew the last ¼" (6 mm) after the dots.

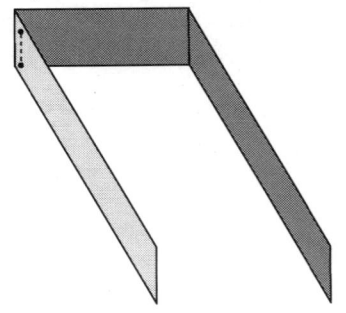

- Match the dots of the other head/foot to the remaining dots on the bed sides.

- Sew the pieces together beginning and ending on the dots.
- The side pieces should be joined to the bed head and foot.

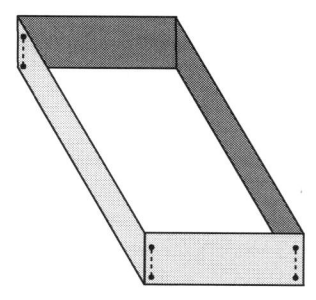

Sewing the Bed Sides to the Bed Top and Bottom

- Finger press the sides seams open. Match the dots on the bed top to the side seam dots.
- Match dots on the head and foot of the bed to the dots on the bed top.
- Match the dots on the bed sides to the dots on the bed top.

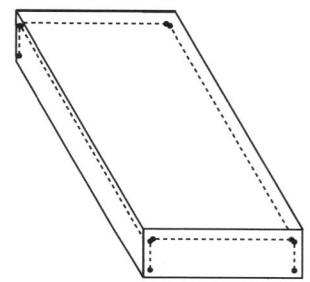

- Pin the bed top to the sides.

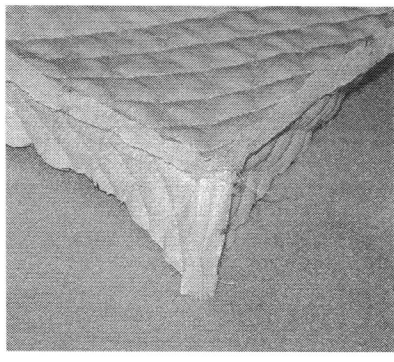

- Sew the bed top to the sides.

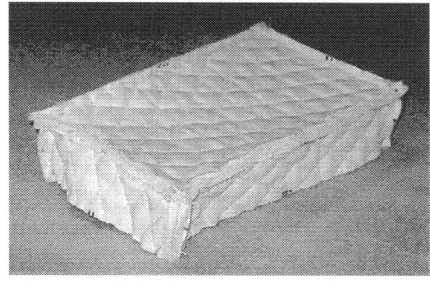

- Match dots of the bed bottom to the sides and foot of the bed.
- Sew sides and foot of the bed to the bed bottom.

- Leave the head of the bed on the bed bottom open for turning and stuffing.

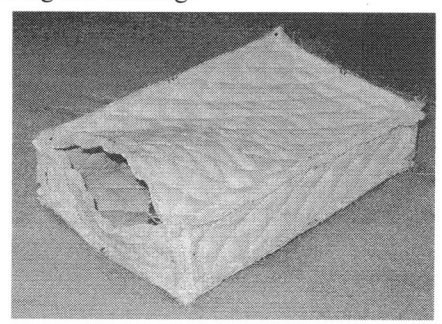

- Turn right side out.

Stuffing the Bed

- Place the foam insert between two layers of plastic canvas.
- Insert the three pieces into the bed.

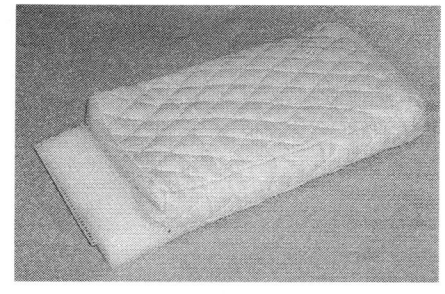

- Slip-stitch or overcast the stuffing opening closed.

The Headboard

Cutting

- Using the pattern, cut out two headboards from quilted fabric.
- Cut out two headboards from quilt batting.
- Trim ¼" (12 mm) off the bottom of the two pieces of batting.

Sewing the Headboard

- Lay the headboard pieces right sides together.
- Lay the quilt batting on top of the two headboard pieces.
- Sew around the headboard.
- Leave the bottom of the headboards open.
- Turn right side out.
- Fold the raw edges of the opening to the inside.
- Close the opening with the slip-stitch or overcasting stitch.

- Topstitch through all the layers over some or all of the quilting stitches on the headboard to stiffen the headboard.

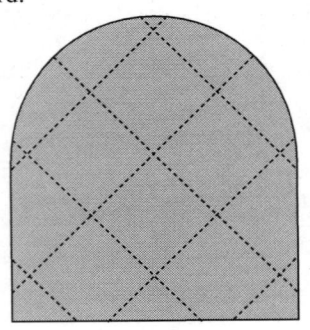

Attaching the Headboard to the Bed

- Sew the bottom of the headboard to the bottom of the bed using the overcasting stitch.

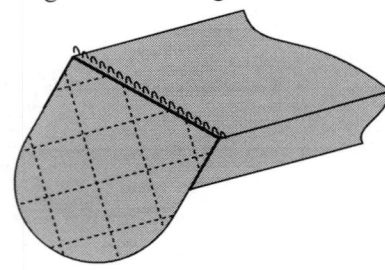

- Sew the headboard to the bed one more time at the top of the bed using the slip-stitch.

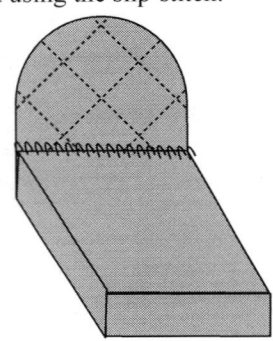

- The bed is ready for the bed clothes.

The Pillows

Cutting and Marking

- Cut one or more pillows and decorative pillows on the fold from fabric.
  - Cut bed pillows 5" by 3¾" (13 cm by 9.5 cm).
  - Cut decorative pillows 5" by 3" (13 cm by 8 cm). You can try a different size if you are trying to get an entire fabric design on the pillow.
- Fold the fabric right sides together to sew the pillows.
  - Fold bed pillows to 2½" by 3¾" (6.5 cm by 9.5 cm).
  - Fold decorative pillows to 2½" by 3" (6.5 cm by 8 cm).
- Measure 1" (2.5 cm) on the sew line on one side of each pillow. Mark a dot on each side of the line. Leave this space open for turning and stuffing.

Sewing and Stuffing Pillow

- Right sides together, sew three sides of the pillow. Leave open the area between the dots that you marked on each pillow.
- Clip the corners.
- Turn the pillow right side out.
- Stuff.
- Sew the pillow closed with the slip-stitch or overcasting.
- Use the slip-stitch to add an applique to decorative pillows if desired.

The Mattress

Cutting

- Cut two mattress from fabric and two mattress from batting.
  - 9¼" by 5¾" (23 cm by 15 cm)

Sewing the Mattress

- Lay the mattress pieces right sides together.
- Lay the quilt batting on top of the two mattress pieces. I like to have the batting on the top so that it will not catch on the feed dogs.

- Measure 2" (5 cm) on the sew line of one short side of the mattress. (See illustration below.) Leave the measured area open. Sew the sides of the mattress. Clip the corners.

leave open

- Turn the mattress right side out.
- Sew the mattress closed with the slip-stitch or overcasting.
- Place the mattress on the bed.

The Pillowcase

Cutting and Marking

- Cut one pillow case on the fold from plain fabric.
- Cut one pillow case trim from printed fabric.
- Mark the notches on the trim and pillowcase.

Sewing the Pillowcase

- WRONG sides together fold the pillow case trim in half long ways, as indicated on the pattern.
- Press.
- Unfold the pillowcase.
- Lay the trim across the right side of the pillow case. Match the notches. All three raw edges should be together.

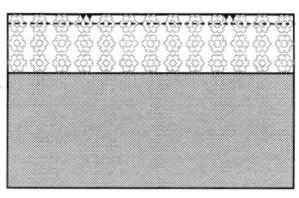

- Sew the trim to the pillow case. Finish the raw edges.
- Flip the trim to the top of the pillowcase.
- Press.

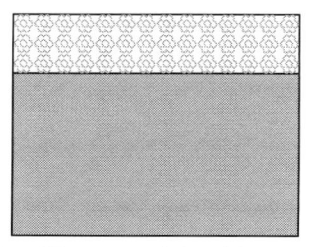

- Refold the pillow case right sides together.
- Sew two sides of the pillow case. Leave the finished edge open.
- Turn the pillow case right side out and insert the pillow.

The Two Fabric Cover

Cutting and Marking

- Cut one cover front and one cover back. You may use different fabrics, if you wish.
  - 9½" by 11½" (24 cm by 19 cm)
- In the middle of one 9½" (24 cm) side of the cover, measure 3¾" (9.5 cm). Mark a dot on either side of the line to keep open for turning.

Sewing the Cover

- Right sides together, lay the cover on top of the cover back.
- Sew all the way around the cover. Leave open the area between the dots.
- Clip the corners.
- Turn right side out.
- Press the cover. Make sure that the seam allowance for turning the opening is pressed to the inside.
- Close the opening with the slip-stitch.

The Hand Quilted Cover

Cutting

- Cut one cover front and one cover back. You may use different fabrics, if you wish.
  - 9½" by 11½" (24 cm by 19 cm)

Sewing the Cover

- Lay the front and back pieces of the cover with WRONG sides touching and RIGHT sides facing out.
- Use pins in a few places to hold the layers together. If you have a large embroidery hoop it works nicely to hold the fabric layers smooth as you sew.
- Use a running stitch to sew parallel lines 1¼" (3 cm) apart.
- Sew another set of parallel lines also 1¼" (3 cm) apart. These lines should run perpendicular to the first set of lines.
- Cover the raw edges with matching double fold bias tape.

Shoes and Purse

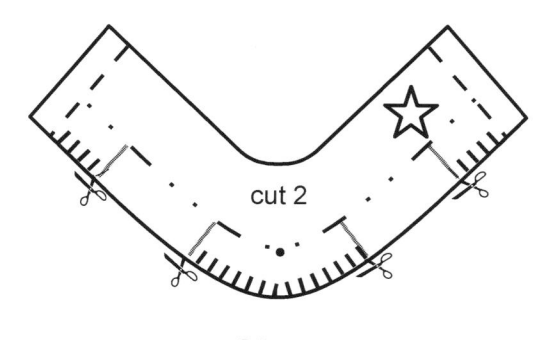

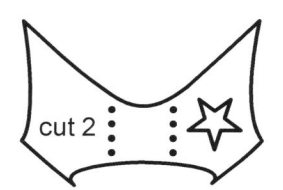

Shoe — cut 2

Sneaker — cut 2

Boot — cut 2 (A, A, B)

Sneaker Overlay — cut 2

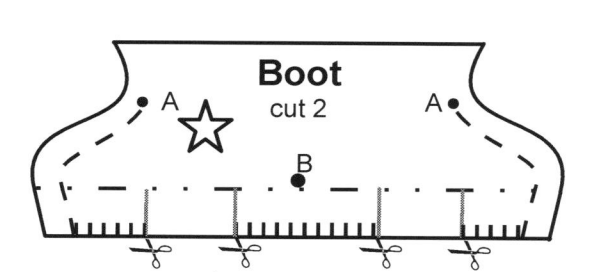

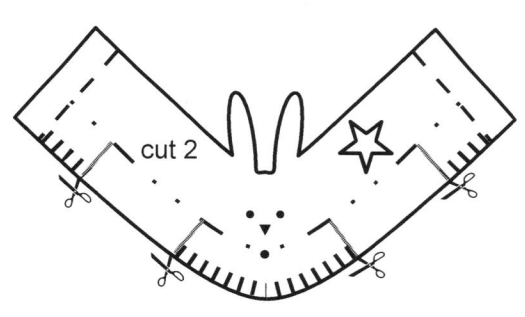

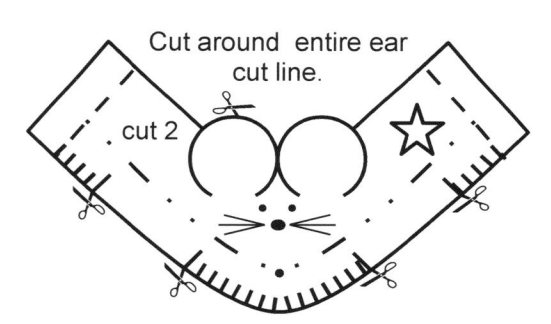

Bunny Slipper — cut 2

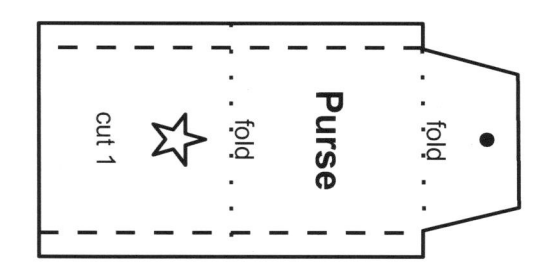

Mouse Slipper — cut 2
Cut around entire ear cut line.

Outer Sole

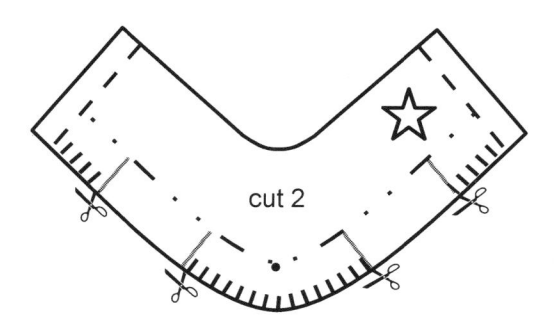

Inner Sole

Purse — cut 1, fold, fold

63

Rain and Sun Hat and Umbrella Cover

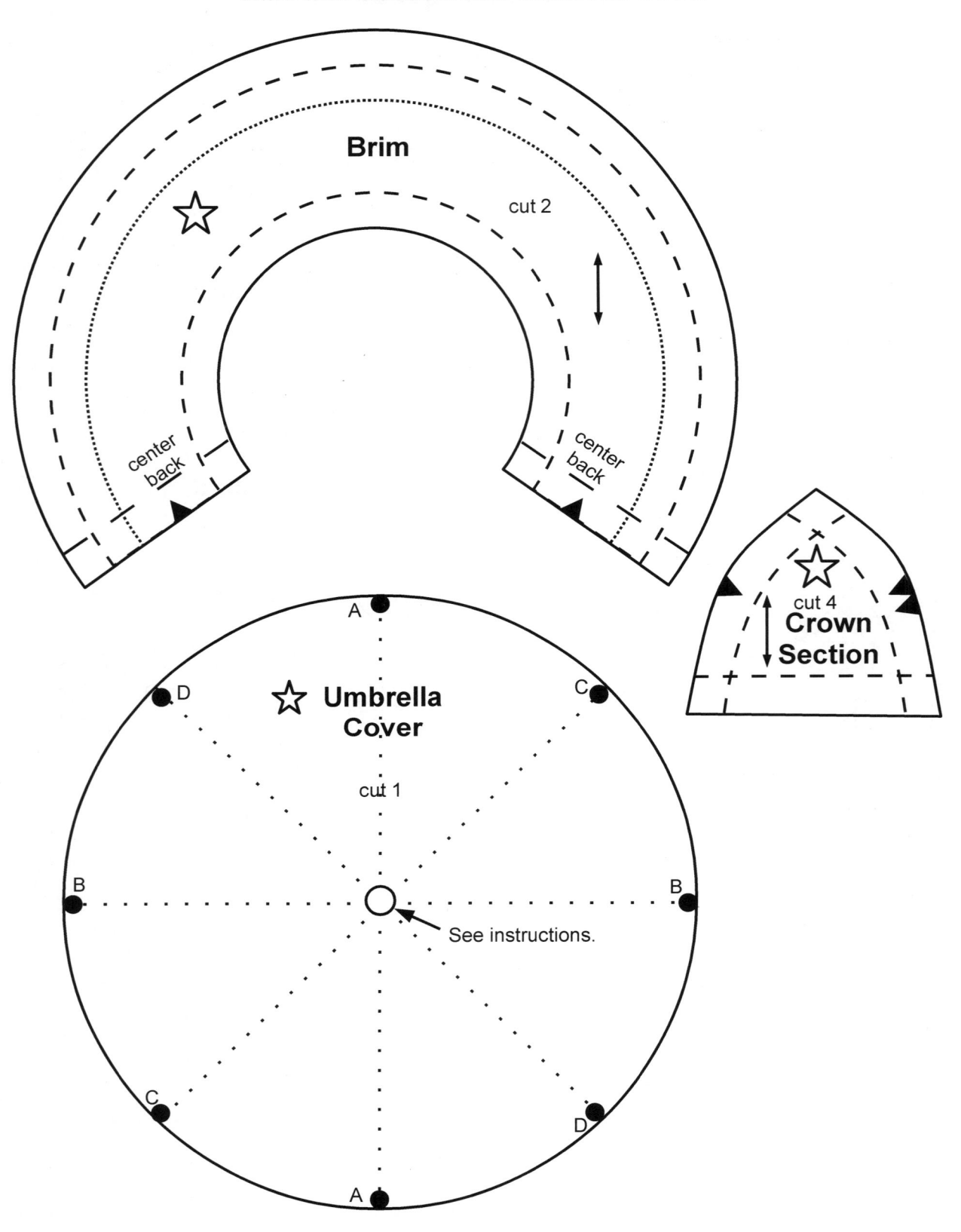

Brim — cut 2

center back

Crown Section — cut 4

Umbrella Cover — cut 1

See instructions.

Backpack

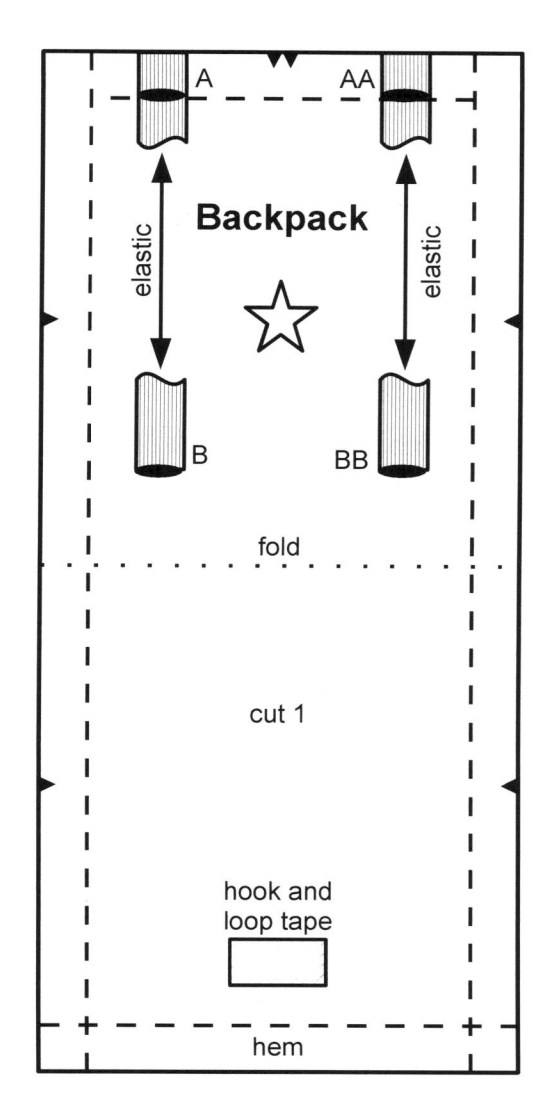

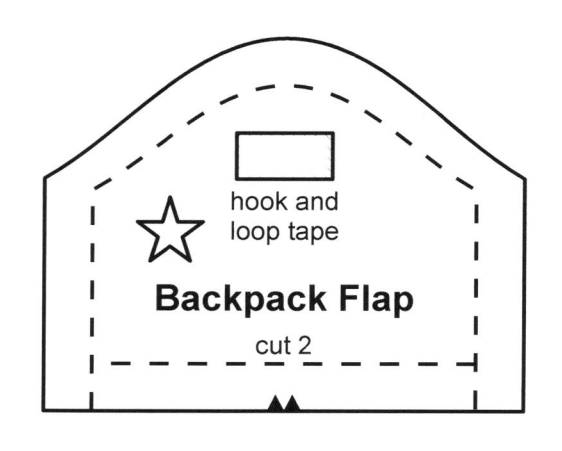

Backpack — cut 1

- elastic A to B
- elastic AA to BB
- fold
- hook and loop tape
- hem

Backpack Flap — cut 2

- hook and loop tape

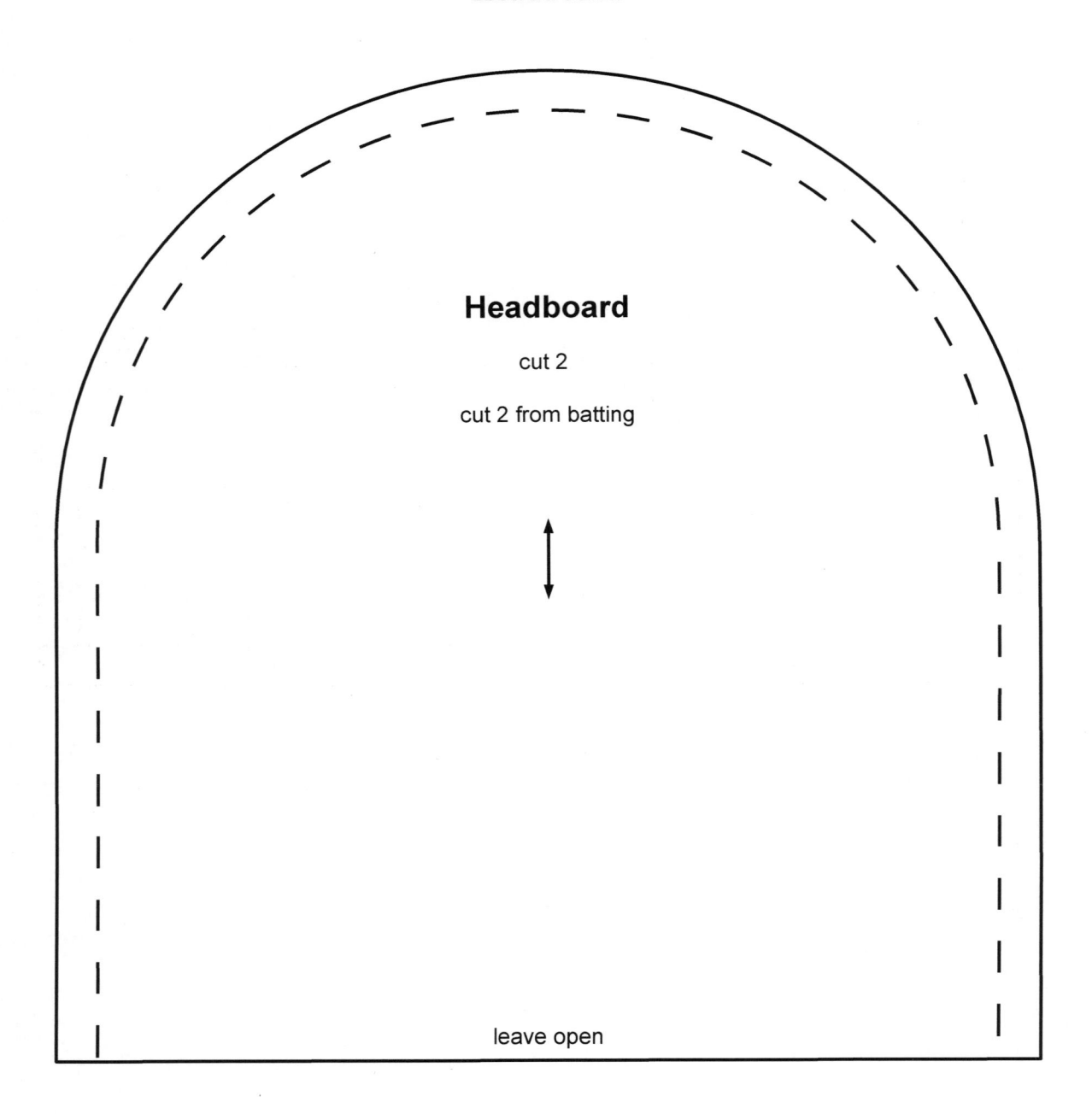

Headboard

Headboard

cut 2

cut 2 from batting

leave open

The Pillowcase

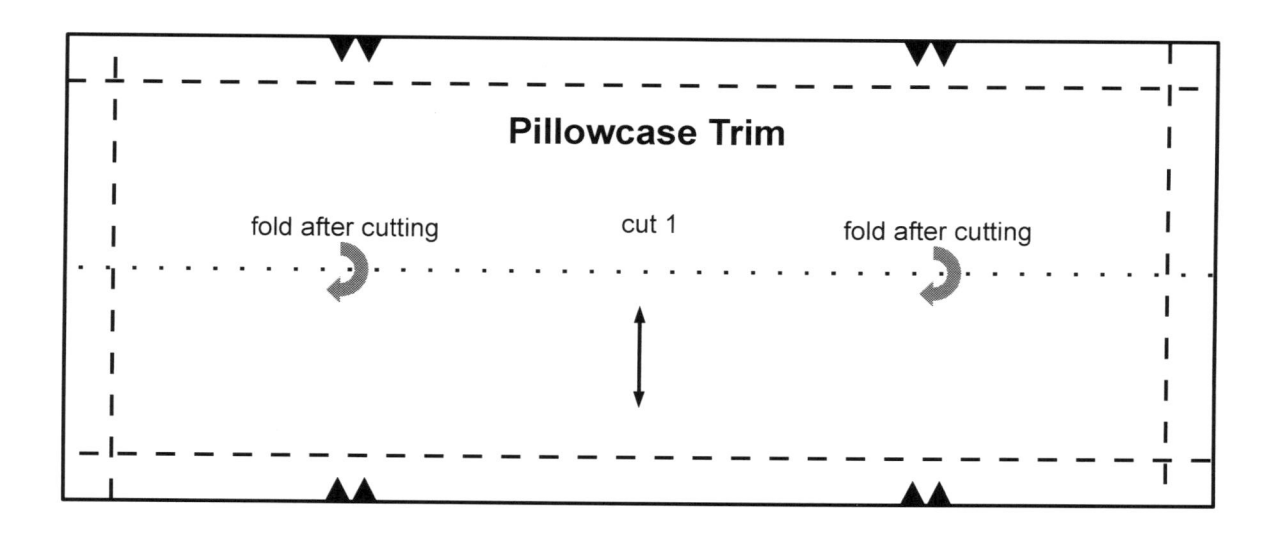

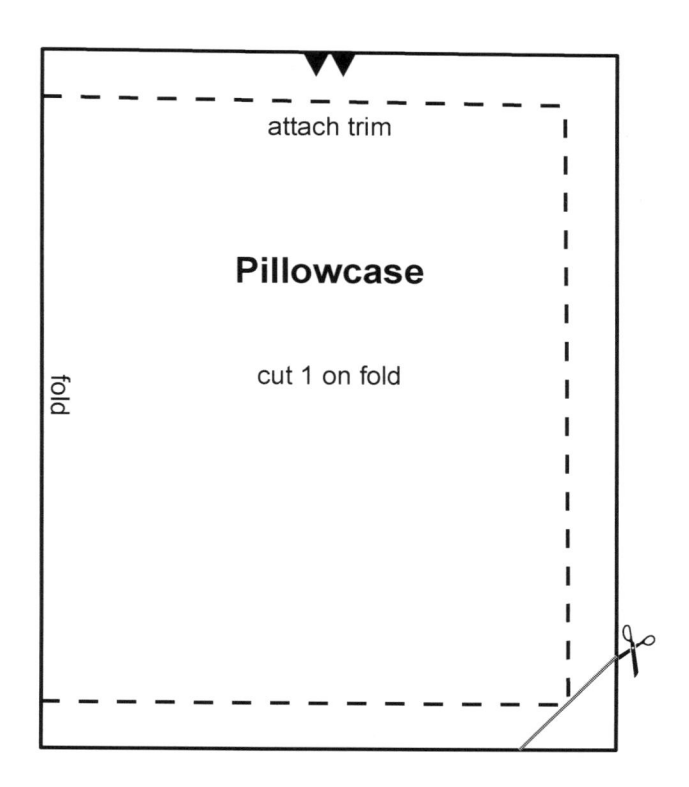

Pillowcase Trim

fold after cutting   cut 1   fold after cutting

Pillowcase

attach trim

fold

cut 1 on fold

Twinkle Doll

Twinkle Doll

Supplies

For Doll Body

- 100% cotton woven fabric in skin color of your choice
- Spoonflower fat quarter print of Twinkle Doll faces and body pattern (optional replacement for skin fabric)
- Thread for sewing doll in slightly lighter color than the fabric
- Darker thread for sewing the toes (optional)

For the Doll Face

If you are using Spoonflower fabric skip this section

- Freezer paper or quilters' freezer paper for printing the face onto fabric (optional)
- Masking tape to help with printing on fabric (optional)
- Prismacolor® peach pencil and thin line air soluble pen for marking
- Boxes of waterproof colored pencils in primary colors and earth tones
- Thin line permanent markers in red, black, brown, and blue or brown for the eyes
- White acrylic paint and a thin brush (eyes)
- Powdered blush (optional)

For Constructing the Doll Body

- Polyester stuffing
- Freezer paper for making arm and leg templates (optional)
- Pairs of ⅜" (9 mm) flat buttons and ½" (12 mm) flat buttons with two eyes for stringing arms and legs
- Unwaxed dental floss
- Seam sealant and wax paper
- Fabric glue stick

For Doll Hair

- Size 4 to 4½ commercial wig (optional)
- If you are making the hair
  - 4 skeins of embroidery floss for hair in the color of your choice
  - Permanent fabric glue (Elmer's® Xtreme® Glue Stick works well)
  - Tear-away stabilizer

Equipment

- An open embroidery foot to use when following sewing lines for arms and legs
- One 2¼" (6 cm) or longer needle for stringing the arms and legs
- Stuffing tools such as a hemostat, chopstick, and an inexpensive paintbrush (use the smooth end)
- A cylindrical object (such as an unsharpened pencil) to keep the neck open while attaching the head
- Doll hairbrush, toothbrush, or fine comb to separate embroidery floss

Head

You may trace the face of the doll onto fabric by hand. You may copy the Face Page included with the patterns directly onto a piece of cotton fabric using an ink jet copier/printer, if you prefer. A third choice is to buy our printed fabric from Spoonflower with a choice of faces printed on the fabric. Of course you are free to create your own doll face, using any method that you like.

Tracing the Face

Suggestions for tracing the face are found in the **Tools, Tips, and Techniques** section of the book under "Marking Fabric." (**Tips** p 92) When you have traced the face, go to the section titled "Coloring the Face" to complete the doll's face.

Printing the Face on Fabric

To print the doll face on cloth, you should have an ink jet copier/printer. I think that it is easier to make a paper copy of the face page rather than copying directly from the book to fabric.

- Cut a sheet of freezer paper 8½" by 11" (letter size).
  - I have found that Reynold's® brand freezer paper works better than house brands.
  - You can now find printable freezer paper, sometimes called quilters' freezer paper, that is cut to the correct size.
  - The patterns are narrow enough that you should be able to use A4 paper if that is more conveniently available than letter size paper. However, I have not tried this myself.
- Cut a piece of woven cotton doll making fabric that is slightly larger than the prepared freezer paper.
- The straight of grain should run down the length of the fabric. Note the straight of grain arrow in the middle of the Face Page.
- Make sure that the fabric is cut straight and is pressed flat.
- Lay the waxy side of the freezer paper on the wrong side of the fabric. The 11" side of the paper should be lined up with the straight of grain. A small amount of fabric should show all around the paper.

- Iron the backing paper to the fabric. Use the cotton setting of your iron. Press down on the fabric while you are ironing. Try to iron out all the air bubbles. Make sure that the fabric is stuck to the backing, especially at edges and corners.

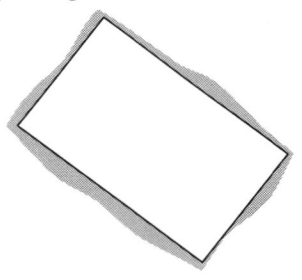

- Trim the fabric to the size of the paper.
- This step is optional. To help the prepared sheet pass smoothly through the printer, I like to fold a strip of masking tape across the end of the sheet that will to feed into the printer first. Fold the tape so that one half of the tape width is on the fabric side of the sheet and the other half of the tape width is on the paper side of the sheet. If you use tape, make sure that the tape is very flat and smooth. Do not leave creases or air pockets. After I smooth out the tape, I sometimes cover it with a pressing cloth and iron it.

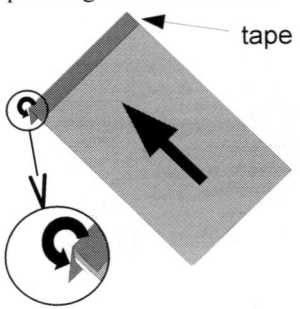

Printing the Face

- Place the prepared sheet in you copier/printer so that the faces will be printed on the fabric side of the sheet.
- Copy the Face Page.
- Peel the tape and backing paper away from the fabric.
- Sometimes the paper backing can be used two or more times.

Completing the Face

- Use waterproof pens and pencils. Follow the directions: "Coloring the Face" below. On two faces on the Face Sheet the features are outlined in black. These outlines will show up clearly on dark skin tone fabric. The other faces have features that are outlined in gray. I have found that it is better to give faces printed in black ink black eye brows and lashes. Faces printed with gray ink can have black or brown brows and lashes.

Coloring the Face

1. Use your printed face outline or trace the face outline and features on fabric.
2. Color over brows and the top arch of the eye with brown or black pen. Fill in irises with blue or brown pencil. Fill in pupils with black pen. Outline irises with blue or brown pen to match pencil color. I have also made a green-eyed face by coloring the iris with green pencil and outlining the iris rim with green pen. Paint the whites of the eyes and eye reflections with white acrylic paint. Notice the placement of the reflection dots on the faces below. The pattern does not indicate the reflection dots' position. You may place them wherever you choose. Add nostril dots with brown pen. Outline nose shadows with orange pencil. Fill in lips with red pencil. Outline lips and lip part with red pen. 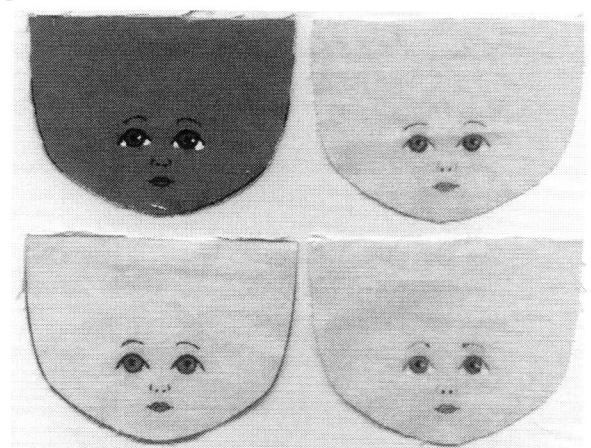
3. The four faces above were printed from a face page and then colored.
4. Even if you are only planning to make one doll, you may want to color all six faces on the fabric Face Sheet. You can experiment with color and line width to find the combination that pleases you.

Making the Head

1. Cut out the face you will be using and head back. Mark the darts on the wrong side of the head back and the inverted T on the right side of the head back. Sew in the darts. Stay-stitch the face and head back ¼" (6 mm) from the top as indicated in the pattern. Right sides together, hand baste the face and head back. Leave the top of the head open. When the sides are matched correctly, the head back will bow out slightly. Machine stitch. Trim the seam to ⅛" (3 mm). (Note that small, sharp embroidery scissors are helpful when trimming and clipping seams.) 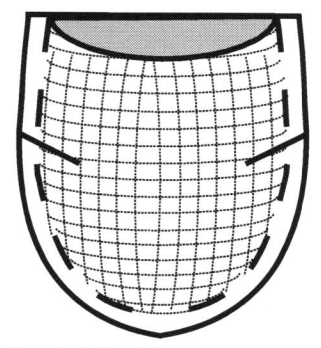
2. Turn the head right side out. Stuff firmly.
3. To close and round the top of the head turn the fabric under at the stay-stitching. Gather this fabric by hand stitching into a circle. Secure the thread and sew around the stitching a second time for strength and to shrink the circle. When you have finished, the circle should be about ⅜" to ½" (9 mm to 12 mm) in diameter. Notice the slight wrinkling around the chin and jaw of the doll head pictured below. The wrinkling can be corrected with stuffing after the neck insertion area is opened in the back. 
4. The small hole at the top of the head and the gathered fabric around it will be covered by the embroidery floss hair or commercial wig.

5. Cut along the lines of the marked inverted T on the back of the head.

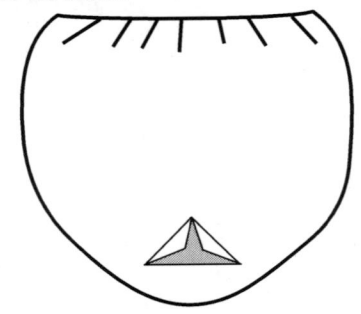

Squeeze a few drops of seam sealant onto a sheet of wax paper and use a toothpick to apply a very small amount of it to the cut edges. Allow the sealant to dry. Fold the cut corners inside the head to form a triangular opening.

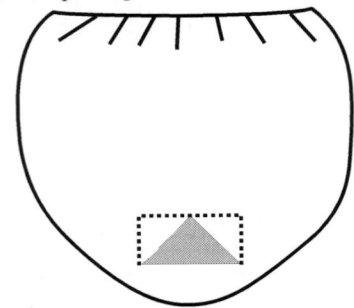

Add stuffing if needed to smooth the face and chin.

Body

Making Body Front and Back

1. Cut out body fronts and backs.
2. Mark dots to show stuffing opening on the wrong side of the body back. Mark the arm string and leg string lines on both the right and wrong side of all body pieces. Make certain that the string lines on the right side of the fabric are a little longer than ¼" (6 mm) so that they will still show up after the body has been sewn together.
3. With right sides together sew body front down the center front line using a ¼" (6 mm) seam.

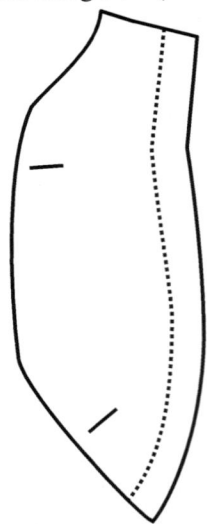

4. Finger press the seams open. (Note that I back stitch all the neck seams and the edges of the stuffing opening.)
5. With right sides together sew body backs together down the center back using a ¼" (6 mm) seam. Leave the space between the dots open for stuffing.

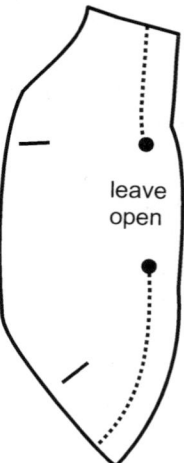

leave open

6. Finger press the seams and the unsewn area between them open.

7. For easier stuffing topstitch around the opening in the center back.

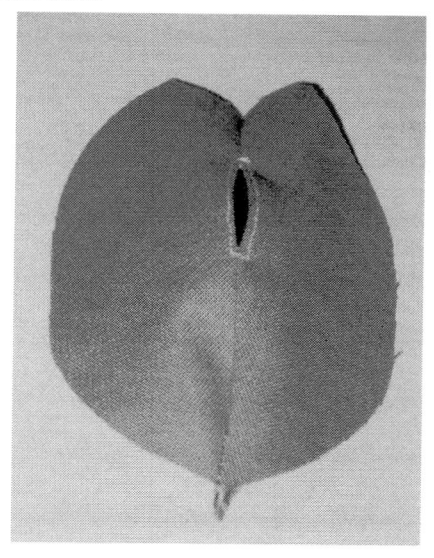

Assembling Body

1. With right sides together pin and baste the body front to the body back. Match the front and back string lines. The edges will meet, but the pieces will not lie flat.
2. Sew all the way around the body using a ¼" (6 mm) seam.
3. Leave the neck open. Clip curves. Turn right side out. (Note that a hemostat makes turning much easier.)
4. Place a cylindrical object through the back opening and into neck to keep the neck open. 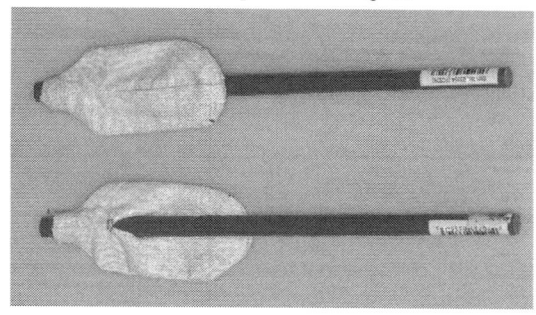
5. Squeeze a few drops of seam sealant onto a sheet of wax paper and use a toothpick to put a very small amount of the sealant around the neck opening. Allow the sealant to dry.

Attaching Head and Body

1. Leave the cylindrical object in the neck to keep it open while sewing. Insert the neck into the prepared opening in the back of the head. Position the head correctly on the body. The nose and mouth should be lined up with the body center front.
2. To stitch the head to the neck using the ladder stitch, take one tiny stitch in the head. Take the next tiny stitch in the neck. Take the third stitch in the head as close as possible to the first stitch. Alternate stitches between the head and neck until you have completely sewn the head to the body. (**Tips** p. **90**)
3. Remove the cylindrical object from the neck and stuff the body firmly. Close the back with an overcasting stitch. (**Tips** p. **90**)

Arms and Legs

Marking and Sewing Arms and Legs

1. Using a peach pencil or air soluble pen, trace two arms and two legs on the wrong side of folded fabric. Mark the spaces to be left open . The peach pencil works on both light and dark fabric. You can use the freezer paper method of sewing around templates if you prefer. (**Tips** p. **92**)
2. If you are using our Spoonflower print of the mini doll pattern, see p. 84 for hints on folding the designated template fabric.
3. Use an open embroidery foot to sew on traced lines. I like to place my Ott-lite® on my machine table to my left to help me see the lines. If you have a needle down option on your machine, it is helpful for this type of sewing. Do not sew on areas of templates marked "leave open," including the toe space on the foot.

Cutting and Beginning to Stuff Arms and Legs

1. Cut out the sewn limbs. Leave a ⅛" (3 mm) allowance in most areas. Leave a ¼" (6 mm) allowance around arm and leg openings. Leave a ¼" (6 mm) allowance at the top and bottom of the foot. The larger seam allowance makes it easier to match the foot seams.

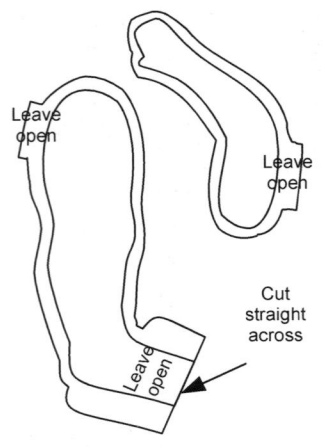

2. Finger press the seams of the top and bottom of the foot open. Bring the top and bottom of each foot together. Match the seams carefully. Sew across the foot using a ¼" (6 mm) seam.

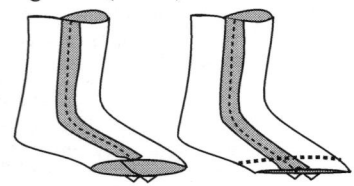

3. Turn the arms and legs right side out. I find a hemostat is very helpful for this step.
4. Begin stuffing the arms and legs firmly. Stop at the stuffing openings.

Marking the Finger Lines

1. For optional fingers, mark finger lines with an air soluble pen on the top and palm of each hand.
2. Make sure to align the finger lines on the top of the hand with the finger lines on the palm of the hand.

Sewing the First Finger

1. Sew the fingers by hand. Thread a needle and tie a small knot at the end of the thread. Start at the inside of one finger line on the palm. You will be sewing toward the finger tip.

2. Push the needle all the way through the palm. Bring the needle out at the same point on the finger line at the top of the hand.

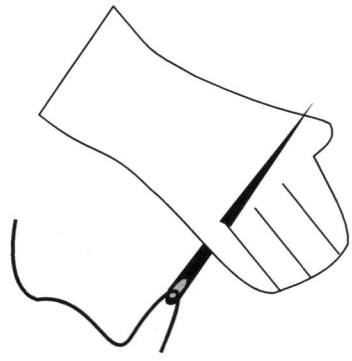

3. Gently pull the thread until the knot goes inside the palm, but does not go all the way through the hand.
4. Make tiny stitches one at a time by moving the needle back and forth through the hand. Always stitch on the finger line.

Moving Between Finger Lines

1. When you reach the tip of the finger send the needle through the hand without catching any fabric to the tip of the next finger line.

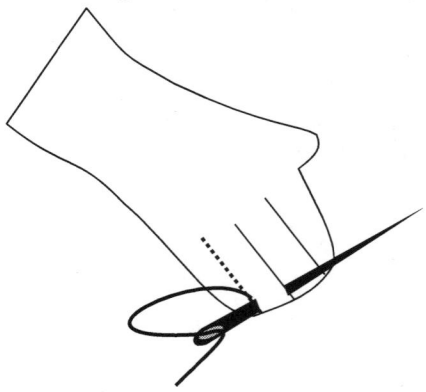

2. Sew the next finger line in the same manner as the first finger line. This time start at the finger tip and sew toward the wrist.

3. When you reach the bottom of the finger line, push the needle through the inside of the hand to the bottom of the last finger line.

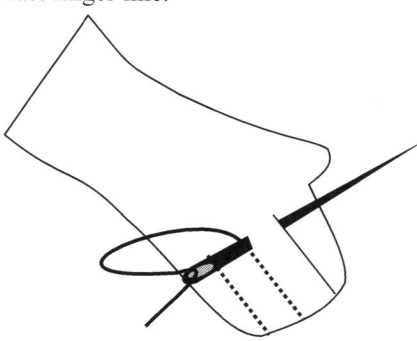

Finishing the Last Finger Line

1. Sew the last finger line. At the tip of the finger go around the last stitch with the needle several times to secure the thread.
2. To hide the thread end, send the needle and thread back through the hand without catching any fabric on either side of the hand.
3. Bring the needle out through the top of the hand.

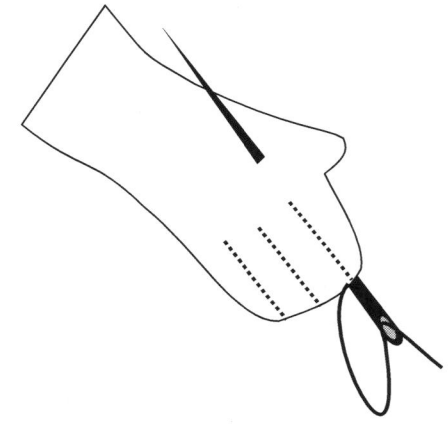

4. Pull the thread tightly before cutting and clip the thread close to the fabric. When the thread is released, the end of the thread will go back inside the hand and be hidden. The toes will be made after the limbs are attached to the body.

Positioning the Arms and Legs

1. Lay the doll body with attached head on a table.

2. Lay the arms and legs on the table so that the parts of the arms and legs that will be touching the body are facing up.

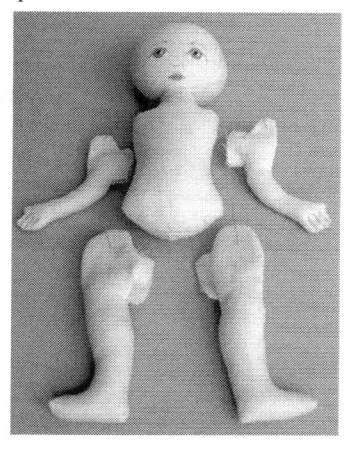

Gluing the Stringing Buttons Inside Arms and Legs

1. Use ⅜" (9 mm) diameter arm buttons.
2. Use fabric glue stick to glue a button inside each arm where the arm will touch the doll's body. Line the button eyes up with the dots indicated on the templates. Make sure that the doll has a left and right arm. Do not tuck the seam allowances of the stuffing openings in until you have finished stringing the doll. (See photo above.) Stick a pin through each button eye while the glue is drying. The pin will show if the eyes are in the correct position. They will also leave small holes in the fabric that will be helpful during the stringing.

3. Follow the same instructions for gluing the buttons inside the legs. Use ½" (12 mm) diameter buttons.

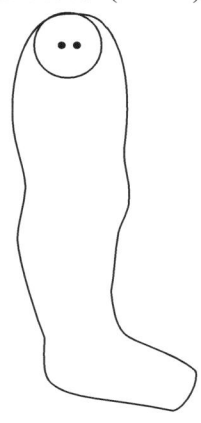

4. Allow the glue to dry.

75

Stringing the Arms and Legs

Inserting the String into the First Arm

1. Cut a 36" (91 cm) length of unwaxed dental floss. Fold it in half to make an 18" (45 cm) length of floss. Use a needle threader to thread a 2¼" (6 cm) or longer needle with the doubled length of floss.
2. Carefully insert the needle into the opening of one arm. Push the needle through button eye A and out the arm.

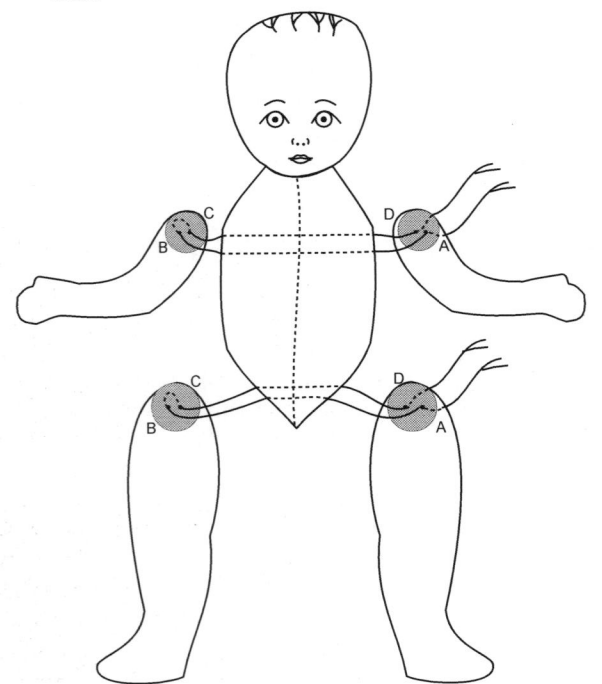

3. Gently pull most of the floss out of the arm. Leave a 3" (7 cm) tail of floss outside the arm. Do not pull the floss tightly. Rest the doll's body and arms on a table while you are working to keep the floss from pulling out of the arm. I usually stand while I am stringing dolls.

Sending the String through the Body Front

1. Insert the needle through the arm string line at the body front.
2. Push the needle all the way through the body front and come out at the second arm string line on the body front.

Looping the String through the Second Arm

1. Insert the needle through the second arm and into button eye B. Carefully bring the needle out of the stuffing opening without catching any fabric.
2. Reinsert the needle into the stuffing opening and insert it into button eye C.

Sending the string through the Body Back

1. Pull the needle out of the arm and insert it into the arm string line on the body back.
2. Push the needle all the way through the body back and come out the second body back arm string line.
3. Push the needle into the first arm through button eye D.

Tying off the Stringing Floss

1. Carefully bring the needle out of the arm through the stuffing opening. Do not catch any extra fabric with the needle.
2. Unthread the needle. Pull the 3" (7 cm) of floss left outside the first arm and unthreaded end of the floss together until the arms are in the correct position on the body.
3. Tie a square knot with the floss and then a second square knot.
4. Cut the floss about 1" (2.5 cm) from the the end of the knots.

Finishing Stuffing

1. Tuck the seam allowances for the stuffing openings and the floss ends into the arm.
2. Stuff around the floss. Finish stuffing arms and close with ladder stitch or overcasting stitch.
3. Attach the legs in the same manner as the arms.
4. Add toes if you like.

Toes

Preparing to Define the Toes

1. Mark the toes on the top and sole of each foot with an air soluble pen. Make sure to align the toe lines on the top of the foot with the toe lines on the sole of the foot.

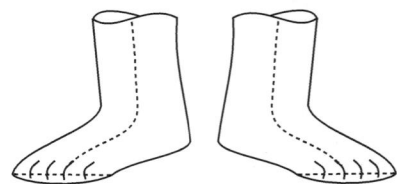

2. Thread a needle and tie a small knot at one end. I use tan thread on a doll with peach skin to make the toes more visible.

Beginning the Sewing

1. Start from the sole of the foot. Put the needle in the foot at the end of the big toe line.
2. Bring the needle out at the top of the foot at the same point on the big toe line.

3. Pull the thread all the way through the foot and gently tug until the knot is inside the foot.

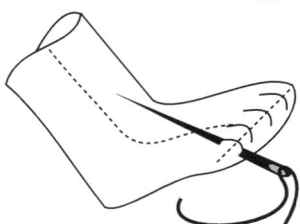

Defining the Toes

1. Insert the needle back in the hole on the sole of the foot where you began making the toe and push it through the line on the top of the foot for the second toe. The thread should have wrapped around the edge of the foot to define the big toe.

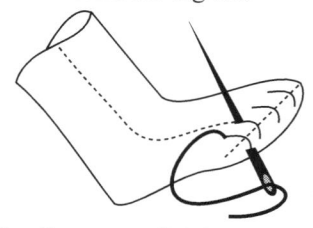

2. Follow the diagram to finish defining the toes.

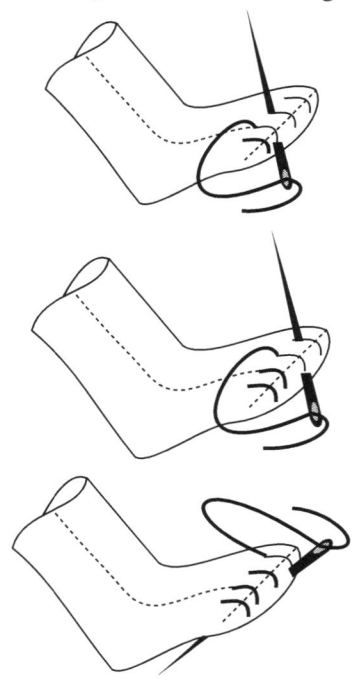

Securing the Thread

1. After you have defined the little toe, take several tiny stitches in the sole at the inside edge of the little toe line to secure the thread.

2. To hide the thread end, send the needle and thread back through the last hole in the foot without catching any fabric on either side of the foot. Bring the needle out through the middle of the sole. Pull the thread tightly before cutting it close to the fabric. When the thread is released, the end of the thread will go back inside the foot and be hidden.

Using a Wig

If you would like to use a wig instead of making braids for Twinkle, purchase a size 4 to 4½ wig. Position it attractively on her head and sew it down by hand.

Hair

Cutting and Sewing the Bangs

1. Trace the stabilizer guides on p. 79 from tear-away stabilizer and cut out. Mark the sew lines and floss lines.

2. Take one skein of embroidery floss and cut it into quarters.

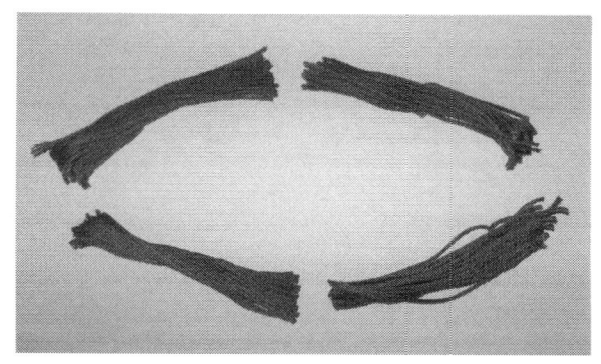

3. The individual strands of floss will be slightly over 3" (7 cm) each. Arrange them on the tear-away stabilizer marked for bangs.

4. Sew the floss on your machine with matching thread where indicated on the stabilizer..

5. Use a toothbrush, doll brush, or fine comb to separate the strands of embroidery floss. Remove the stabilizer.

Attaching the Bangs to the Head

1. Pull out about 24" (60 cm) of floss from one of the remaining skeins of embroidery floss. Separate two strands from this length. Use the separated strands to sew the bangs to the head by hand.
2. The bangs floss should cover the forehead above the eyebrows. The floss behind the bangs should cover the top and back of the head including the hole surrounded by gathering stitches. This back hair will be covered by the floss that will be parted to make braids. 
3. Pin bangs to head and hand sew along the seam line.
4. Use fabric glue to hold the floss to the top and back of the head. Use a small amount of glue under the bangs at the top of the forehead. Leave most of the bang floss loose.
5. Carefully trim any floss at the back of the head that does not lie neatly.

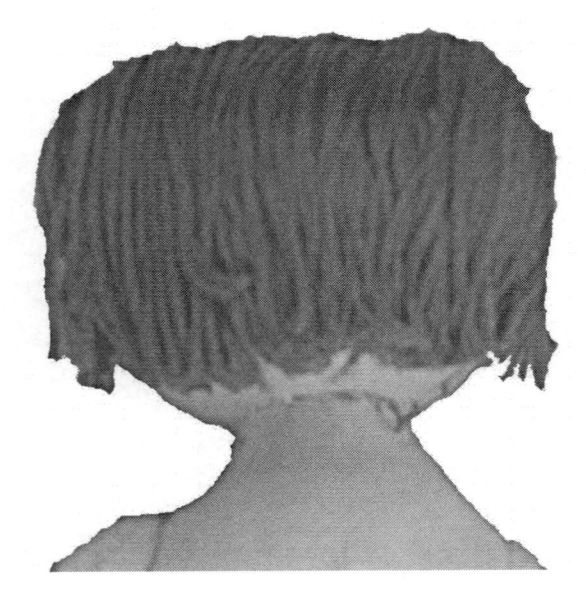

Cutting and Sewing the Part

1. Use three skeins of floss.
2. Cut each skein in half. 
3. Place the braid tear-away stabilizer under the middle of the floss. Each strand of floss is about 12" (30 cm) long. Arrange the floss on the stabilizer so that the middle fold of the floss is on the sew line of the stabilizer.
4. Sew through the middle of the floss so that there is about 6" (15 cm) of floss on each side of the machine stitching. 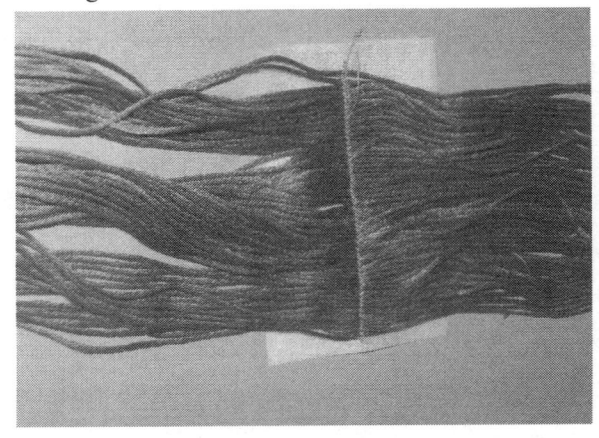
5. Use a toothbrush, doll brush, or fine comb to separate the strands of embroidery floss. Remove the stabilizer.

Attaching the Part to the Head

1. Arrange the floss so that the bangs seam is hidden and the part runs down the middle of the head.
2. Pin in place. Use two strands of the reserved floss to sew the part in place.

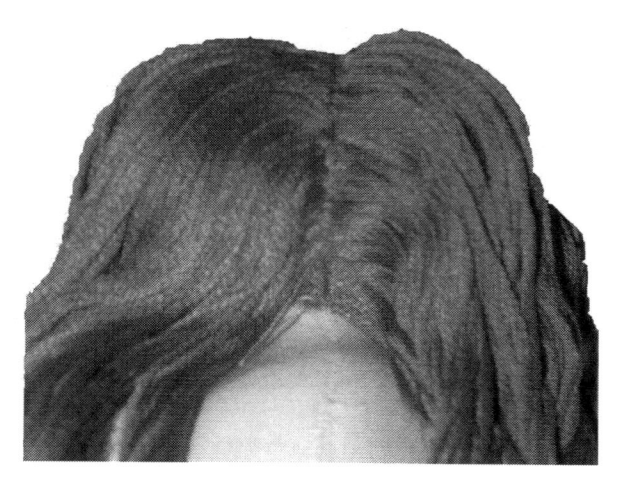

Adding Blush

If you would like pink cheeks on your doll, add powdered blush on the finished doll. Put a small amount of blush on each cheek with a small brush or cotton swab. Rub the color in with a makeup sponge or dry wash cloth.

Stabilizer Guides

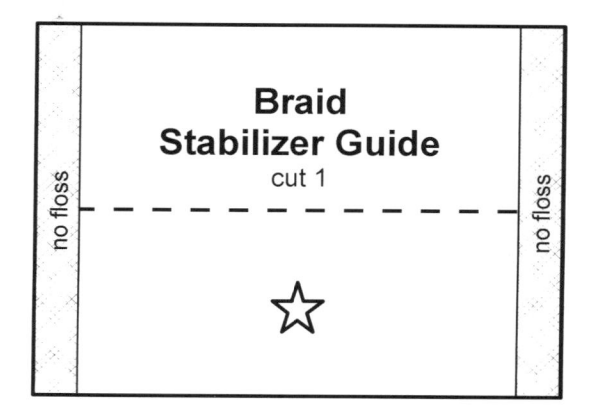

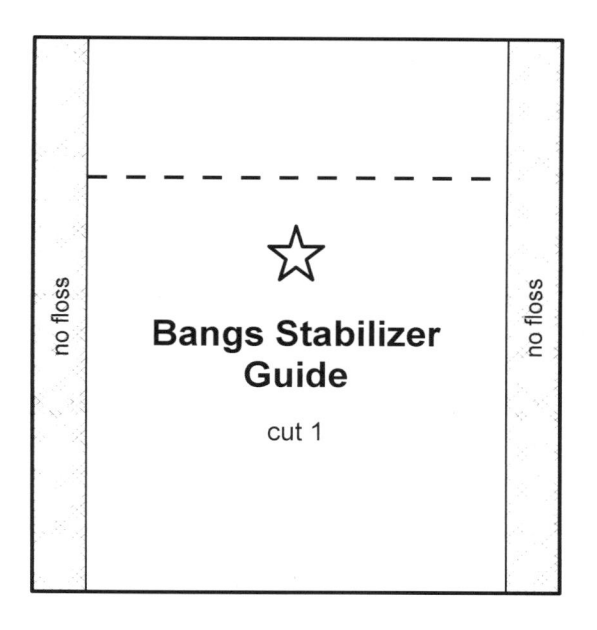

Braid Stabilizer Guide
cut 1

Bangs Stabilizer Guide
cut 1

Making the Braids

1. Make a pony tail on each side of the head. Use the reserved floss to sew each pony tail in place.
2. Leave the hair in pony tails or braid each pony tail and secure with the rest of the floss. 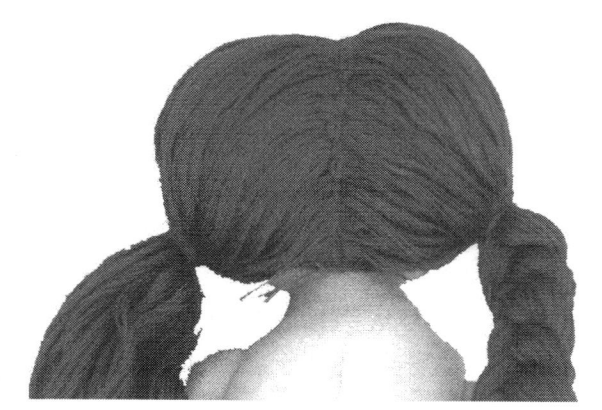
3. Trim the floss below the braid ties as needed.

Face Page

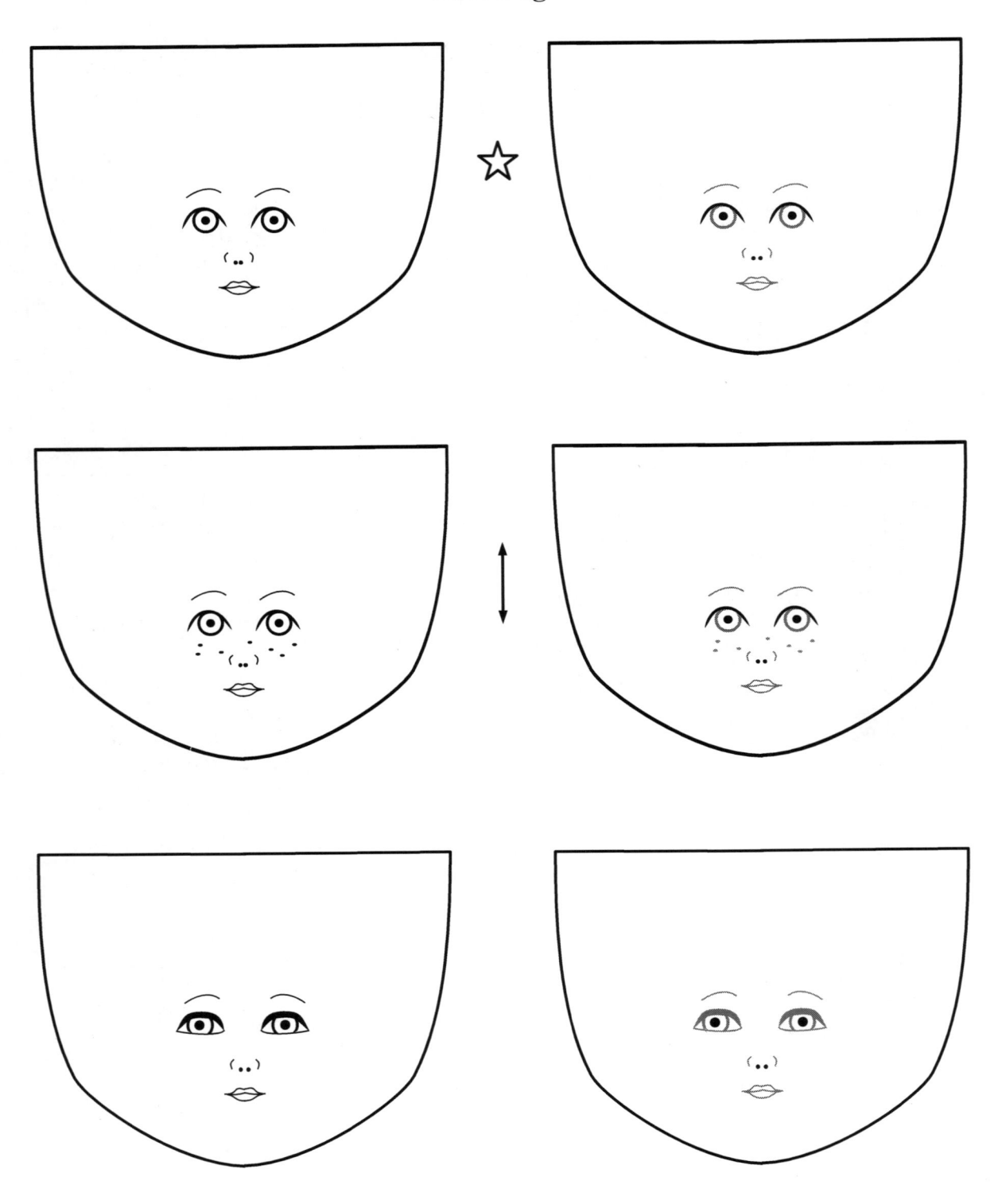

80

Twinkle Doll

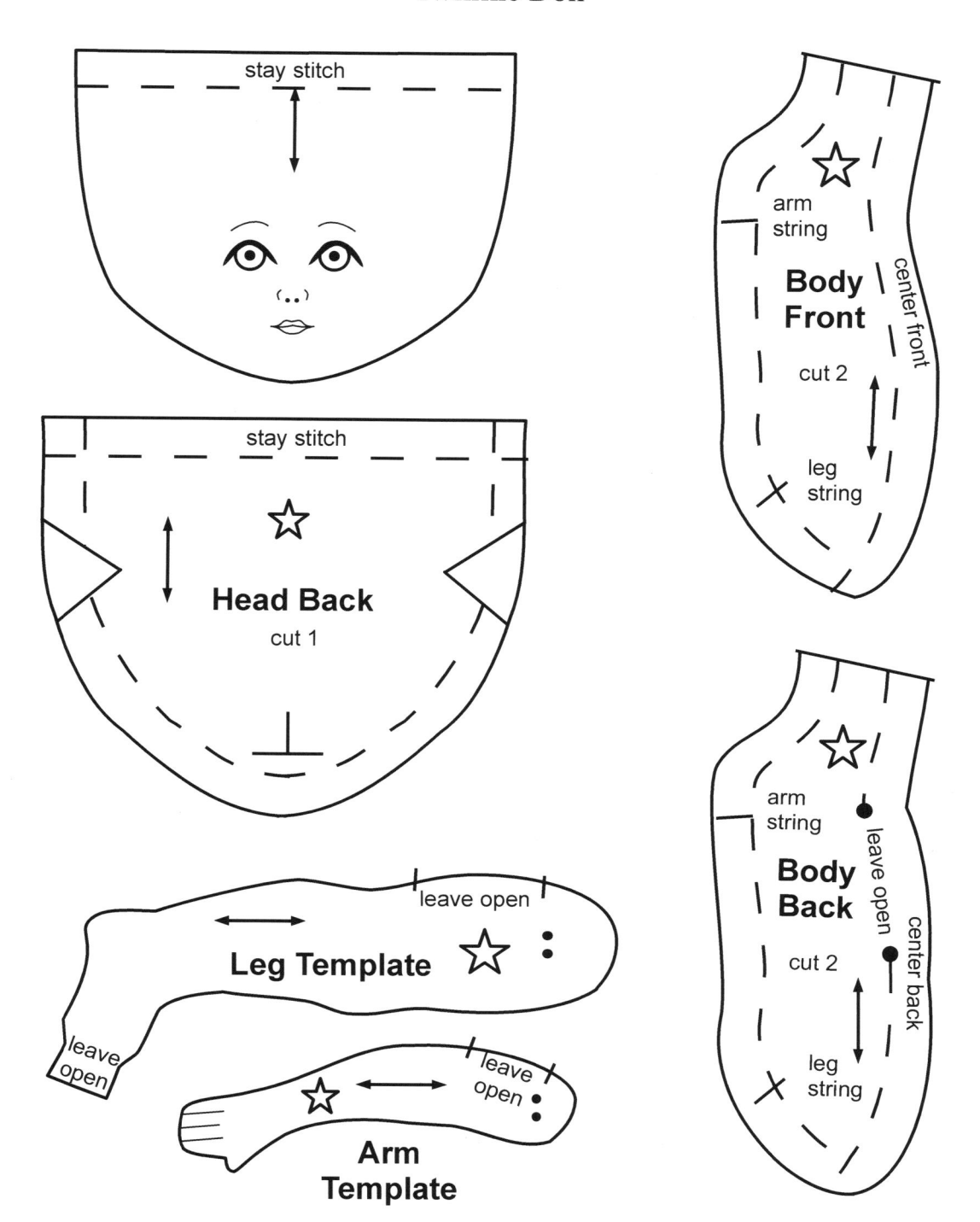

81

Sewing for Mini Dolls
www.sherralynsdolls.com

Spoonflower® Custom Printed Fabric

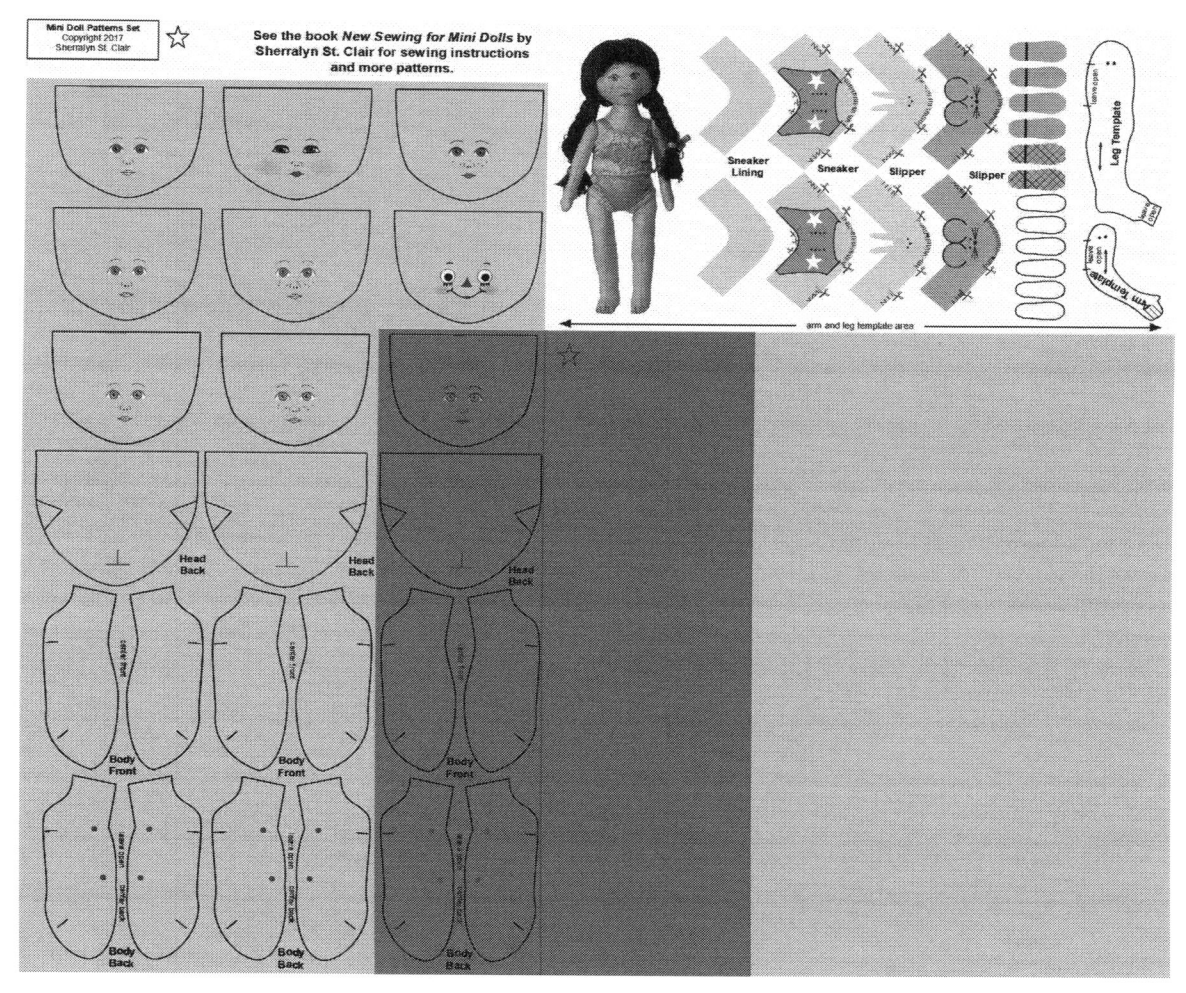

    Traditional doll makers select their own fabric and sew up the doll from scratch. That's the assumption for most of the instructions in this book. If that is your approach, then you can skip this chapter. However, if you would like to try something different, Sherralynsdolls has made custom printed fabric available through the Spoonflower® company. I find that Spoonflower's fabric is of high quality and you get the convenience of not having to draw the doll's face yourself. I find that the having the patterns pre-printed is a time saver. However this custom printed fabric is more expensive than most generally available fabric and there is a wait while Spoonflower fills your order. So many doll makers will prefer the traditional approach. If you want to try something new, continue reading.

    You can order a fat quarter of printed fabric to make three Twinkle mini dolls. The fat quarter will make one dark skinned doll with brown eyes and two lighter skinned dolls with a choice of faces. You can also make a pair of sneakers and two pairs of slippers from prints on the fabric. If you are interested in making sneakers and slippers, but not dolls, you can order a sneaker swatch from Spoonflower to make three pairs of sneakers and one pair of slippers. I suggest choosing Kona cotton for both the doll and shoe projects.

    To see the fabric, go to Spoonflower's website. Use their search bar to select fabric and search for sherralynsdolls. Look through our fabric selections to find the mini doll fabric. If you are interested in custom prints, please check back occasionally. We hope to continue adding fabric to our Spoonflower collection.

Making the Twinkle Mini Doll from Printed Fabric

Preparing to Use the Fat Quarter

- I suggest that you carefully cut the template fabric away from the rest of the fat quarter, before cutting out the dolls' heads and bodies. You will need all of the template fabric for the dolls' arms and legs.

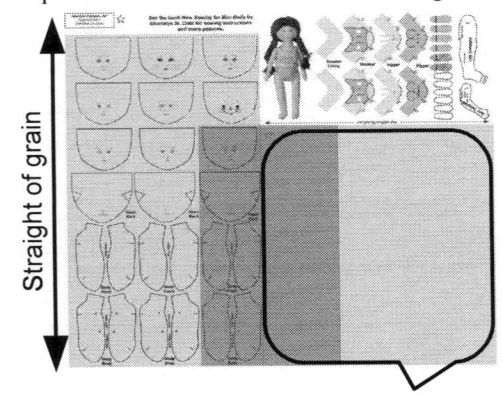

- You can cut out the arm and leg templates, if you like.
- Use fusible webbing to glue the templates to light cardboard.
- Cut them out and later you can trace around them onto fabric or freezer paper.

Using the Mini Doll Book Instructions

- Check Supplies and Equipment on p. 69 beginning with *For Constructing the Doll Body*.
- Start following the instructions for constructing the doll on p. 71 beginning with *Making the Head*.

Using the Template Fabric

- When you reach **Arms and Legs** p. 73 it is time to use the fabric from the template area of your Spoonflower fat quarter.

- You can cut the template into three equal strips following the straight of grain, so that you have one strip of dark fabric and two lighter strips, or you can leave the fabric in one larger piece.

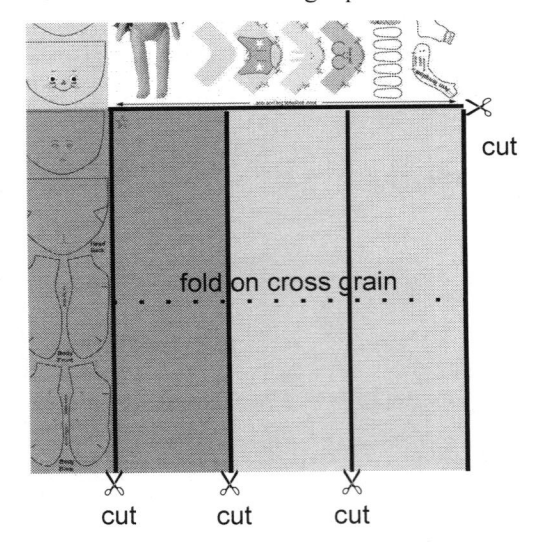

- Fold your template fabric in half on the cross grain.
- Here is a suggestion for arranging the arm and leg templates on the template fabric, if you have cut your fabric into three pieces.

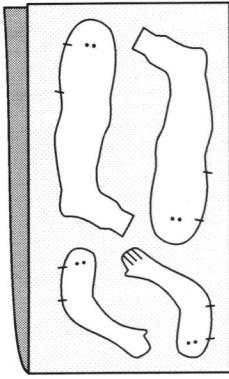

- You can use the fabric templates if you fused them to cardboard, or you can trace the templates in the book. Follow the instructions in the **Arms and Legs** section of the book p. 73.

Making the Sneakers from Printed Fabric

Cutting and Adding Fusible Webbing

- Cut out sneakers and sneaker linings.
- Back lining fabric with fusible webbing.
- Back the soles and insoles with fusible webbing.
- Fuse the soles and insoles to light cardboard. I like to use the cardboard found in commercial fat quarters.

Attaching Sneaker Lining

- With right sides together, sew sneaker to sneaker lining all the way across the top of the sneaker. Use a ⅛" (3 mm) seam. The webbing side of the lining should be

on the outside and should not be touching the sneaker fabric.
- Clip curve at the three places indicated on the seam that you have just sewn.

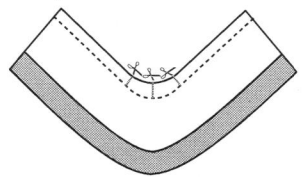

- Remove the backing from the fusible webbing.
- Turn the sneaker right side out so that the raw edges of the seam that you have just sewn are hidden. The webbing side of the lining should now be touching the wrong side of the sneaker fabric.
- Press to fuse the lining to the shoe.
- Go to *Adding Laces* p. 51 and follow the instructions in the shoe section to finish the sneakers.

Making the Slippers from Printed Fabric

Cutting and Adding Fusible Webbing

- Cut out slippers.
- Back slippers with fusible webbing.
- If you have not done so already, back the soles and insoles with fusible webbing.
- Fuse the soles and insoles to light cardboard.

There are two ways to assemble the slippers. The printed slipper images can be used as either the outside of woven cloth slippers or as the lining for felt slippers.

Making a Woven Cloth Slipper

- Remove the paper backing from the fusible webbing.
- Iron the slippers to a small piece of fabric.
- Cut out the lined slipper.
- If you do not wish to embroider the facial features, skip that section and continue sewing the slippers. Otherwise, follow the directions starting with *Making Facial Features* under **Slippers** p. 50.

Making a Felt Slipper

- Remove the paper backing from the fusible webbing.
- Iron the slippers to a small piece of felt in the color of your choice.
- Cut out the lined slipper.
- Follow the directions starting with *Making Facial Features* under **Slippers** p. 50.
- Embroider the facial features on the felt, using the printed slipper lining as a reference to locate the features.
- Continue constructing the slippers using the book's directions.

Sewing for Mini Dolls
www.sherralynsdolls.com

Tools, Tips, and Techniques

APPENDIX

The following hints have been taken from my blog and revised for the sake of continuity. Occasionally a note in my instructions will refer you to topics in this section. Some of the short cuts that I use are not traditional methods. If you prefer traditional methods, please use them.

Sewing Tools..88

Stitches..89

Marking Fabric..92

Finishing Raw Edges...93

Casings..94

Special Details..95

Closures..95

Sewing Tools

Sewing Machine

- It is much easier to sew small doll clothes and cloth dolls if you use a sewing machine with controllable speed. A sewing machine that only has a fast speed is hard to maneuver while you are sewing short seams and small curves.
- A zigzag stitch is a must for sewing knits. Zigzagging is an easy way to finish seams on tiny doll clothes.

Basic Sewing Basket

I like sewing gadgets. I keep them in boxes and drawers all over my sewing room. If I were furnishing a sewing basket with basic sewing tools, I would list: dressmaker scissors, an assortment of pins and a pin cushion, an assortment of hand sewing needles, a thimble, and a tape measure.

- It is important that scissors are sharp and well made. I have both Gingher® and Fiskars® dressmaker shears. I can recommend either pair. When sewing for small dolls, I also like Singer® 6½" Sewing Scissors with Pink and White Comfort Grip. It is easier to cut small shapes with these small size scissors.

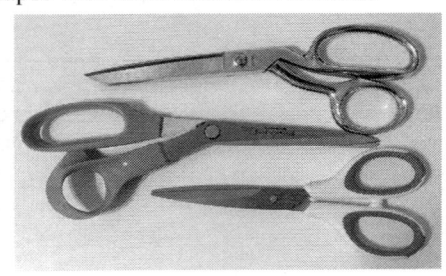

- I usually use glass head silk pins, but sometimes I use silk pins with a smaller metal head. I have an over sized tomato pin cushion and now a globe pin cushion made from the free pattern offered on my website.

- I have an assortment of hand sewing needles. Different sewing jobs need different size needles. The needle I use most often for hand sewing is a size 8 embroidery needle. For some jobs I may choose a longer or thinner needle. Occasionally I list an unusual size needle under equipment at the beginning of a pattern.
- Not everyone uses a thimble, but I can't get along without one.
- Along with my regular width tape measure I have a narrow tape measure made to use in dollmaking.

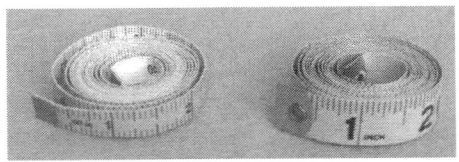

Basic Ironing

It is as important to press seams between sewing steps in doll dressmaking as it is to press while making larger projects. Basic Ironing equipment is essential to sewing.

- Steam iron
- Full size ironing board
- Spray water bottle for moistening fabric if you are not using steam in your iron

More Sewing Tools

Here is a list of other sewing tools that are useful. Occasionally I list one of these tools under equipment at the beginning of a pattern.

Sewing Machine Tools

- Open embroidery foot

I use this foot when I am sewing around a traced shape or freezer paper. The foot's openness makes the sewing area easy to see.

- Ott-lite®

I have an Ott-lite® on my sewing table. I use it along with my open embroidery foot to stitch a traced shape.

- Patchwork foot

This foot was made for quilters, but it is great for sewing ¼" (6 mm) and ⅛" (3 mm) seam allowances on doll clothes.

More Sewing basket

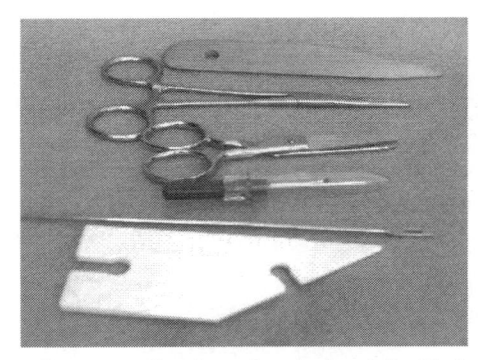

The picture shows a collection of tools that I find helpful.

- There are two different point turners in the picture.
  - The one at the top of the picture is helpful when turning curved pieces.
  - The bottom turner is helpful for defining sharp angles.
  - Both turners are helpful for defining points.
- The second tool from the top is a hemostat. It is helpful for turning small fabric pieces and stuffing dolls and toys.
- I use my small scissors for clipping seams and delicate trimming.
- A seam ripper is very useful to me. I need it more often than I like to admit.
- The bodkin makes it easy to insert elastic into a casing.

More Ironing

- Doll clothes ironing board

I have a small ironing board made for pressing doll clothes that I find very useful. It makes pressing little sleeves and hems easier.

- A sleeve roll

A sleeve roll is sometimes a good choice for pressing small sewing projects, because small pieces may be pinned to it. I push the pins straight down into the roll as if it were a pin cushion.

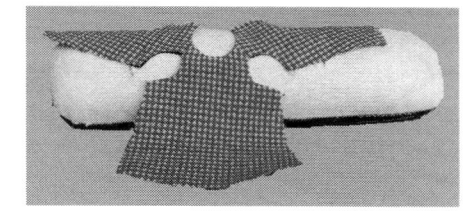

- Finger pressing

Sometimes in dollmaking the only pressing equipment that you need is a finger or two.
  - To finger press a seam open, spread the seam and run your index finger or thumb down the stitch line. Put enough pressure on the stitch to encourage the seam to stay open.
  - To finger press a crease in the fabric pinch the fabric between your finger and thumb at the spot where you want the crease to begin. Pull the fabric through your finger and thumb along the line to be creased. If you are not satisfied with the crease, repeat the pinch and pull process.

Stitches

Machine Stitches

- Stay-stitching
  - Stay-stitching is usually sewn on the stitching line of a single layer of fabric.
  - It is used to prevent fabric from stretching.
  - It is used as a guide for folding or clipping fabric.

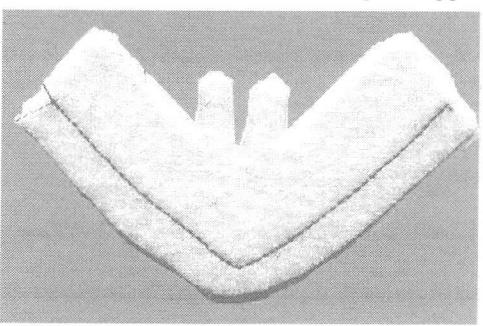

- Topstitching
  - Topstitching will be visible on a finished garment.
  - Use the edge of the presser foot or a seam guide to produce a straight stitch.
  - Match the thread color to the fabric or choose an interesting contrast.

- Gathering stitch
  - Sew two parallel rows of long stitches and pull the bobbin threads until the fabric is gathered to the desired length.
  - Check the fabric to see if the stitches can be removed from the fabric without leaving small holes. Then one row of gathering stitches may use a ⅜" (9 mm) seam guide even though the joining seam will be ¼" (6 mm). Remove the visible gathering stitch after the joining seam has been sewn.

- Zigzag stitch
  - Joining knit fabric
    - Use zigzag stitches to join knit fabric. I have not had success using a serger to join very small knit pieces.
    - Use a fairly wide zigzag stitch to join knits. Set the zigzags to be fairly close together, but not a satin stitch.

- If your zigzag is not as wide as the seam allowance, you may trim the seam.

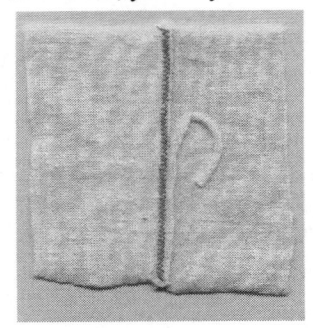

  - Sewing lace to knits with the zigzag stitch
    - Lay the lace on the right side of the fabric.
    - If the lace will extend above or below the fabric, overlap the raw edge of the knit with the lace heading.

    - If the lace will lie on top of the fabric make the heading even with the raw edge.
    - Stitch a narrow almost satin stitch on the lace heading.

Hand Stitching

One stitch is defined as the needle going into and coming out of the fabric.

- Running stitch

Several stitches are made with the needle before the thread is pulled through the fabric.

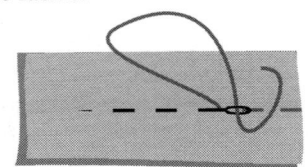

- Basting stitches

Basting stitches are running stitches used to hold fabric together so that it can be sewn with a machine stitch.

- Hand gathering

Hand gathering stitches are running stitches that are pulled so that the fabric is gathered over the thread.

- Slip-stitch
  - A slip-stitch is an almost invisible stitch. It is a good stitch to use when putting in a hem.
  - Finish the raw edge of the garment to be hemmed.
  - Press in the hem. For these small doll patterns the hem is usually ½" (12 mm).
  - Use a few pins to hold the hem in place.
  - Check the length on the doll before continuing.
  - Fold the finished edge back about ⅛" (3 mm). 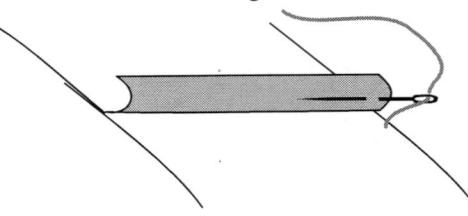
  - Take about an ⅛" (3 mm) stitch through the folded back edge. Pull the thread through the fabric.
  - Catch two or three threads and take a small stitch on the part of the hem that will be visible on the dress.
  - Take the next stitch in the folded back edge. For these small hems the visible stitches should about ¼" (6 mm) apart.

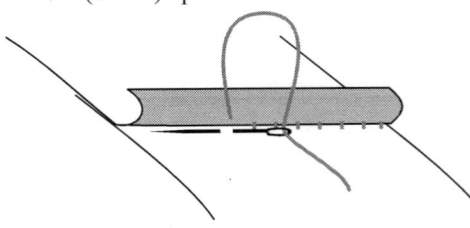

- Ladder stitch

In doll patterns and doll crafting magazines the invisible hand stitch used in doll construction is called the ladder stitch. In embroidery books the ladder stitch is a decorative stitch that looks like a ladder. The dollmaker's ladder stitch is similar to the slip-stitch, but it is done on the outside of the doll.

  - Using the ladder stitch to connect the doll's head to the body
    - Insert the neck into the opening in the head.
    - Use a few pins if you like to hold the two parts together. I usually just hold the two together as I sew.
    - Take a small stitch in the head.
    - Pull the thread through each stitch as you take it.
    - Take the second stitch in the neck.
    - Go back to the head for the next stitch and make it very close to the first stitch.
    - Continue back and forth.
    - Take only one stitch at a time. Pull the thread completely through with each stitch.

- Keep the stitches very close together. You should take between fifteen and twenty stitches per inch.

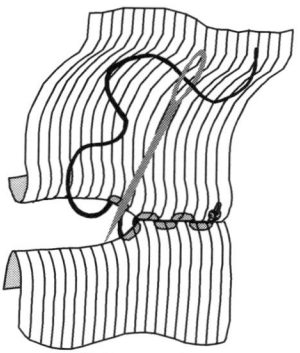

Picture courtesy
Dover Publications
"Easy to Make Story Book Dolls"
by Sherralyn St. Clair

- Sewing arm and leg stuffing openings closed with the ladder stitch
  - Finish stuffing each piece.
  - Tuck the raw edges of the stuffing opening inside the arm or leg.
  - Hold the edges of the stuffing opening together as you sew.
  - Do not overlap the edges as you sew.
  - Take a small stitch on one side of the opening.
  - Pull the thread through each stitch as you take it.
  - Take the second stitch on the other side of the opening.
  - Go back to first side for the next stitch and make it very close to the beginning stitch.
  - Continue back and forth. Keep the stitches very close together. You should take between fifteen and twenty stitches per inch (between 1 and 2 mm apart).
- Overcasting stitch
  - Using overcasting to close a body back stuffing opening
    - Start sewing at the top of the stuffing opening on the left side of the opening. Hide the thread knot by inserting the needle into the top of the stuffing opening and bringing it out on the left side.
    - Make a stitch straight across the opening to the right side.
    - Make the second stitch going right to left slightly slanted. The second stitch in each pair will be inside the closing, so that the visible stitches go straight across the stuffing opening.
    - Continue back and forth keeping the outside stitching straight

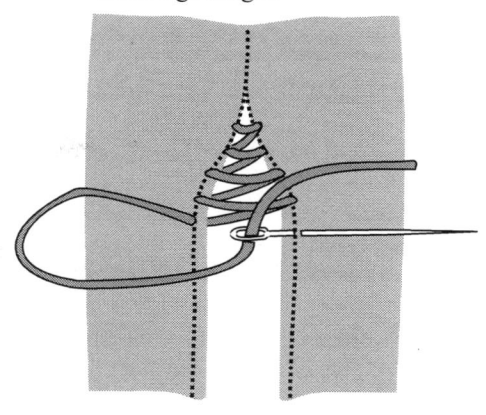

    - Pull the stitches taunt as you sew. The above figure shows loose stitches to illustrate thread placement.
  - Using overcasting to close an arm or leg
    - Finish stuffing each piece.
    - Tuck the raw edges of the stuffing opening inside the arm or leg.
    - Hold the edges of the stuffing opening together as you sew.
    - Sew both sides of the opening together with each stitch.
    - Keep the stitches small and close together.

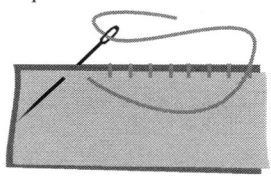

- French knot

The French knot is the embroidery stitch used for the bunny's and mouse's eyes on the slippers. The books I have read have different opinions on the number of times to wrap the floss around the needle while making the stitch. One book says only one wrap. One book says one or two. Another book says two or three wraps. I decided to use the average of two wraps for the bunny's eyes. To make thicker French knots, use more strands of floss.

  - Bring the needle to the right side of the fabric slightly to the right of the point marked for the French knot.
  - Pull all the floss through the fabric until it stops at the knotted end.
  - Hold the needle close to the marked point and wrap the floss around the needle twice.

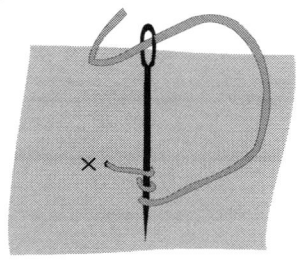

- Insert the needle through the point marked on the fabric.

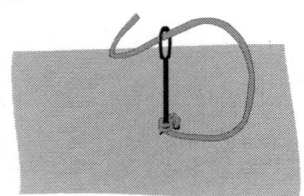

Marking Fabric

First choose a pen, pencil, or other method to mark your fabric pieces. Then choose the method to use for transferring the pattern markings to the fabric. You can find other more traditional methods for marking fabric in sewing handbooks.

Choosing Pens and Pencils

- Use a thin line air soluble pen when marking on the right side of the fabric. I find that the thicker air soluble pens are not precise enough for marking small size sewing projects. Mark with this type of pen just before sewing, because it disappears quickly. Sometimes the markings will last a few hours or a few days zipped in an air tight plastic bag. The time the marking lasts depends on the age of the pen and the amount of humidity in the air.
- For marks on the wrong side of the fabric and marks for embroidery designs, I like to use Prismacolor® pencils. They wash out easily.
- If you prefer more traditional marking methods, you can purchase tailor's chalk in various colors, or try a marking wheel and transfer paper.

Tracing Markings

- Hold the pattern and fabric up to a window to trace markings. This method is easier if the pattern and fabric are held to the window with drafting tape. (I think masking tape is too strong.)
- A clear plastic box picture frame works fairly well when tracing pattern markings. It should be propped up at an angle rather than resting flat on a table. Another solution is to have a battery powered light under the plastic box. Light should be behind the pattern that you are tracing.
- My favorite tracing method is a light box or table. I bought a small inexpensive one years ago. Larger ones may be fairly pricey. I use a small amount of drafting tape to hold the pattern and fabric to my light box.

Using Freezer Paper

- Draw around your template on a scrap of freezer paper.
- Cut out the drawings.
- Place the drawings, waxy side down on the folded fabric.
- Iron.
- Sew around the paper.
- Remove the paper.

Clipping Fabric

- Cut out the small notches in the seam allowance that are used to help match fabric pieces. 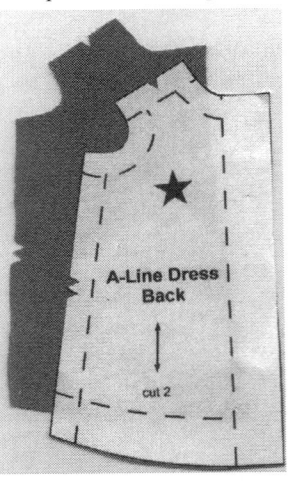
- You can make a small clip in the middle of each notch if you prefer.
- You can also color in the notches with a marking pencil rather than clipping them at all.

Cutting out Parts of a Paper Pattern

- Darts
  - Rather than tracing darts you can copy a second pattern piece.
  - Cut the dart shape out of the pattern.
  - Place the pattern on the fabric piece to be marked.
  - Trace the dart where it belongs on the pattern.

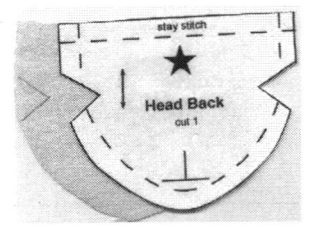

- Dots
  - Pull a pin with a small metal head through the dot on the paper pattern.
  - Put the pattern on the fabric to be marked.
  - Use a pen or pencil to mark the fabric through the hole in the pattern.

Finishing Raw Edges

Serger

- Finishing two raw edges together
  - Sew the seam with a straight stitch on a sewing machine.

  - Serge using only three spools of thread. This method produces a narrow finished seam and a small stitch connecting the fabric pieces. Serge close to the machine stitching so that the serger knife will trim the seam to about ⅛" (3 mm). Note that the bottom of the sample has not been serged to show how the serger knife has narrowed the seam.

  - Add a drop of seam sealant on the stitching at the beginning and end of each line of serging.
  - Press the seam to one side.
  - Small curves such as those on sleeves and necklines of doll clothing are difficult to do with a serger.
- Finishing single edges in hems and casings
  - Use only three thread spools to make a narrow finish.
  - Sew near the edge so that the fabric is not cut with the knife.

  - Turn up the hem the desired amount and slip-stitch.

  - For hems in A-line garments add a machine gathering stitch next to the finished edge.

  - Pull the gathering thread until the hem lies flat against the skirt and slip-stitch.

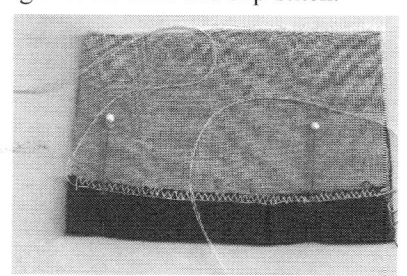

Zigzag Stitch

- Finishing two raw edges together
  - Sew the seam with a straight stitch.

  - Set the zigzag stitch about ⅛" (3 mm) wide.
  - Make the zigzags close together, but not a satin stitch.
  - Zigzag close to the straight stitch so that there is about an ⅛" (3 mm) raw edge.
  - Trim the seam close to the finished edge.

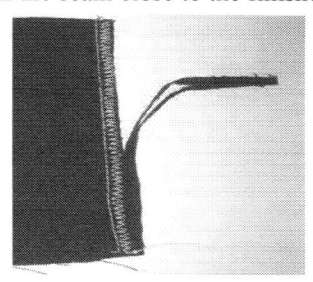

  - Press the seam to one side.

- Finishing single edges in hems and casings

93

- Sew near the edge to be finished.
- Turn up the hem the desired amount and slip-stitch. 
- For hems in A-line garments add a machine gathering stitch next to the finished edge.
- Pull the gathering thread until the hem lies flat against the skirt and slip-stitch.

Pinking Shears

- Small curves such as those on sleeves and necklines of doll clothing are difficult to cut with pinking shears.
- Pink the seam close to the raw edge. The measurement from the peak of the pinked edge to the stitch should be almost ¼" (6 mm).
- These seams may be pressed open unless they are inside an elastic casing. 
- The pinked edges may be pressed in the same direction so that the machine stitching is visible inside the garment. The edges must be pressed in one direction if they will be inside an elastic casing.

Using a Seam Sealant to Finish Seams

- Lay the cut pieces that you want to treat on a sheet of wax paper.
- Squeeze a few drops of seam sealant onto the wax paper. I have tried applying the sealant directly to the fabric, but I always ended up with too much on the edges. Too much sealant makes the fabric edges stiff and difficult to sew through.
- Use a toothpick to apply a small amount to the outside edges of the fabric pieces.
- To make the sealed edges softer, after the sealant has dried, soak the treated pieces in a bowl of water. After five or ten minutes remove the fabric from the water. Blot the pieces and let air dry. Press. The fabric is soft and easy to sew. This soaking step is optional.
- These seams may be pressed open unless they are inside an elastic casing.

Casings

- To insert elastic into doll clothes casings I always use ⅛" (3 mm) elastic and my favorite bodkin. 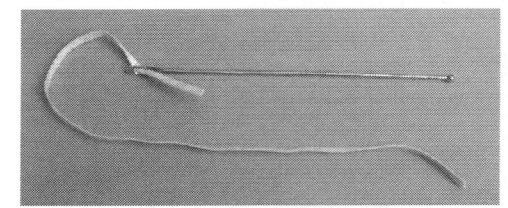
- Use your whole length of elastic. Do not cut it until it is secure on both sides of the casing. Use a bodkin to pull the elastic through the casing.
- If a seam is inside the casing, the two seam edges should have been finished together and pressed to one side. The bodkin should travel over the stitching first and then over the two seams.

- Pull the elastic through the casing with the bodkin.
- Release the elastic from the bodkin and secure the released end to the casing by sewing through it several times.

- Check the pattern instructions for measurement. Gather the casing fabric over the elastic to the desired length without stretching the elastic.
- Try the garment on to check the size.
- Secure the second side of the elastic to the second casing opening by sewing through it and the casing several times.

- Cut off the excess elastic.

Special Details

Square and Rectangular Pockets

- Fold a small scrap of matching or contrasting fabric in half right sides together.
- For each pocket needed trace around the pocket template onto the folded fabric. You can use the freezer paper method, if you prefer. (**Tips** p. 92)
- Sew all the way around the pocket shape.
- Trim to an ⅛" (3 mm) seam allowance all the way around the pocket.
- Pull the two fabric sides apart.
- While the sides are separated, cut a small hole in one side of the pocket.

- Turn the pocket right side out through the hole that you have just cut.
- Press or finger press.
- Mark the pocket placement on the right side of the garment fabric with air soluble pen.
- Place pockets over placement markings.
- Make sure that the cut side is touching the garment fabric and the uncut side is visible.
- Pin in place or use sewing glue stick to hold it in place.
- Topstitch around three sides of the pocket. Leave the top of the pocket open.

Appliques

- If you are using a commercial applique use handstitching, a small amount of fabric glue, or Elmer's® Xtreme® Glue Stick to hold it down.
- To make an applique from a small design cut from fabric:
  - Roughly cut the design from fabric.
  - Iron light fusible inner-facing to the back of the fabric.
  - Carefully cut out the design.
  - Seal the cut edges with seam sealant and allow to dry.
  - Use machine zigzagging, fabric glue, or Elmer's® Xtreme® Glue Stick to hold it down.
  - You can use fusible webbing instead of fusible inner facing and press the design onto the garment, if you prefer.

Lace

- Follow the patterns instructions when applying lace edging.
- Refer to the figure below for a definition of a lace's heading and edge.

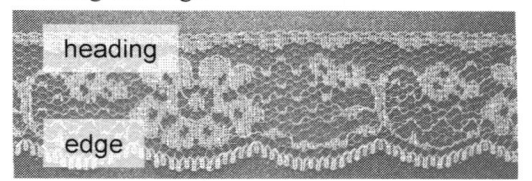

Closures

Closing the Back with Hook and Loop Tape

I like to close garments for small dolls with short pieces of hook and loop tape. In this method the left and right sides of the closing will be side by side like a zipper closing rather than overlapping like closings with buttons or snaps. I do not use the overlap method for hook and loop tape in these patterns, because the overlapped closing is too thick on such small dresses.

- Use your favorite method to finish each side of the opening.
- Press each finished side of the opening ½" (12 mm) to the inside.

- Take a 1" (2.5 cm) length of ¾" (18 mm) wide hook and loop tape. The hook side and the loop side of the tape should be fastened.
- Split this tape in half lengthwise so that there are two 1" (2.5 cm) lengths of ⅜" (9 mm) tape.

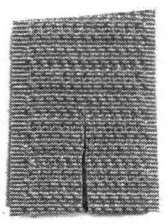

- Separate the tape into the hook and loop sides.

- Take the hook side of one of the tape pairs and lay it face up partly under the right side of the opening at the top of the opening. About ¼" (6 mm) of tape should stick out of the opening and about ⅛" (3 mm) of the tape should be under the fabric edge of the opening. The bumpy hook side of the tape should be touching the fabric at this ⅛" (3 mm) overlap.
- At the edge of the right back opening stitch through the fabric and the tape.
- Lay the first piece of loop tape completely inside the left side of the back opening. The loops should be out and the smooth side of the tape should be against the fabric.
- Stitch down the tape through the fabric.
- At ⅛" (3 mm) from the bottom of the tape, pivot on the needle and stitch a few horizontal stitches.
- Pivot on the needle again and stitch back up the tape.

- For garments that need a second strip of hook and loop tape measure ½" (12 mm) down from the first piece of loop tape and sew the second piece of tape in the same manner as the first tape.

- I like to use snag free Velcro®. The snag free variety sticks to itself, so you don't need to worry about hook and loop sides. To use this type of tape, split a single 1" (2.5 cm) length of tape in half lengthwise so that you have two narrow 1" (2.5 cm) lengths. Use one piece in place of the hook side and one piece in place of the loop side in the above instructions.

Closing the Back with Snaps

If you prefer an overlapped closing, use small snaps.
- Press under ½" (12 mm) at back left closing and ¼" (6 mm) at back right closing.
- Overlap right over left ¼" (6 mm).
- Check fit on doll before applying snaps.
- Use two to four snaps to close dress.

Other Books by Sherralyn St. Clair

Sewing for Large Dolls-Full size Patterns for 18" Doll Outfits

This book is a collection of patterns for large 18" (46 cm) dolls. The book includes full size patterns and detailed sewing instructions for the Kitty cloth doll and her outfits. In addition to Sherralyn's Dolls Kitty, the outfits will fit American Girl® dolls, Springfield® Collection dolls, and other 18" dolls. Measurements are given in both US and metric units.

The patterns include: Nightgown and nightcap; A-line Dress, and Jacket; Pants, Shorts, Skirt, and T-shirt; Ballgown and Classic Dress; Shoes, Slippers, Sandals, Sneakers, and Six Styles of Bedroom Slippers; as well as Kitty Cloth Doll, Camisole, and Panties.

Sherralyn's Tools, Tips, and Techniques is included.

Learn to Sew for Your Doll - A Beginner's Guide to Sewing for an 18" Doll

If you would like to teach a special child how to sew, this book presents a series of skills in a learning sequence that takes the new seamstress from the first use of a sewing machine through making an attractive wardrobe for a doll. The book gives the student a place to start and then builds on the initial skills.

This book includes instructions and full size patterns for 18" doll clothes. Measurements are given in both US and metric units.

Skills taught include: pattern reading and cutting, machine stitching, finishing seams, gathering, sewing casings, topstitching, hemming, and attaching closures.

Sew a Small Doll and Her Clothing-Full Size Patterns for 7½" Florabunda and her Outfits

This book is a collection of patterns for the small Florabunda dolls (7.5" or 19 cm). The book includes full size patterns and detailed sewing instructions for the Florabunda cloth doll and her outfits. In addition to Sherralyn's Dolls' Florabunda, the outfits will fit Madam Alexander®'s Wendy, Vogue®'s, Modern and Vintage Ginny, as well as Lillian Vernon®'s doll.

The patterns include: Nightgown, Smock Top, and Two Tiered Skirt; A-line Dress, Jacket, and Bloomers; Pants, Shorts, Skirt, and T-shirt; Ballgown and Classic Dress; Shoes, Slippers, Sandals, Sneakers, and Boots; as well as Florabunda Cloth Doll, Camisole, and Panties.

Sherralyn's Tools, Tips, and Techniques is included.

Easy-to-Make Storybook Dolls-A "Novel" Approach to Cloth Dollmaking

This unique guide to making 14" cloth dolls offers patterns for the eternal optimist, Pollyanna, as well as Dorothy from *The Wonderful Wizard of Oz* and Mary of *The Secret Garden*. Perfect for beginners, this manual will also appeal to more experienced dollmakers.

All three characters use the same basic doll body and accessories such as hats, shoes, and slips. Dorothy's wardrobe, based on descriptions of her clothing in Oz books, comprises six dresses and a nightgown. Mary's ensemble includes five dresses, a coat, and a housecoat; and Pollyanna's costumes consist of six dresses and a gown. Extras include Dorothy's green spectacles and Toto the terrier; a bed cover, and a pillow for Mary; and Pollyanna's pets, Fluffy the cat and Buffy the dog.

Sherralyn's Dolls

Visit my web site at www.sherralynsdolls.com to get more fun out of your pattern books. Here's some of what you can find there.

Patterns

The Patterns page contains patterns for doll clothes, accessories, and cloth dolls of various sizes. Many of the patterns in my books can be purchased separately for download from this web page.

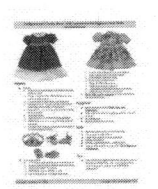

You can also find a free sundress pattern for three sizes of small dolls, a free sewing tips booklet, and free miniature quilt block patterns.

Florabunda's Page

This page is kid friendly with a music video and fun surprises.

It has free sewing and craft projects that let kids make accessories for themselves and their dolls.

My free stories can inspire kids to use their dolls for creative play.

My Books

On My Books page you can find color versions of outfits from the books. E-mail me whenever you have sewing questions.

Blog

Check my blog page for sewing hints and thoughts on sewing. Feel free to leave a comment and start a discussion.

Made in the USA
Middletown, DE
02 July 2018